A Whole New Ball Game

A Whole New Ball Game

Gerald Williams

Marshalls

Marshalls Paperbacks
Marshall Morgan & Scott

3 Beggarwood Lane, Basingstoke, Hants, UK.

ISBN: 0 551 01056 8
Phototypeset by Input Typesetting Ltd, London SW19 8DR
Printed in Great Britain by
Richard Clay (The Chaucer Press) Ltd,
Bungay, Suffolk

To Alan Godson, who believes it's more important that he tells people the truth than that he might be ridiculed or rejected; to Lesley, who somehow manages to be the loving wife of this rarity; and to their three Neddies, who climb all over my bed when I stay and enjoy baptising hamsters.

Contents

Introduction

Someone told me he thought X, a very famous sportsman indeed, was probably a Christian.

It didn't surprise me. From what I had read of him, seen of him interviewed on television, and from the warm feeling I always had for him on the few times we had met, it seemed quite possible that he was.

Obviously, he was very much in control of himself. He was well-mannered, modest without being self-effacing, intelligent and good-humoured.

So when we unexpectedly found ourselves plundering the same plate of sandwiches in the television village of instant offices behind the Centre Court at Wimbledon one day, I asked him: 'Are you a Christian? A friend tells me you are.'

'Well,' he replied, not content with a slick or cosmetic explanation, 'well, yes, I suppose I am. I mean, I certainly support Christian ethics: you know, the Ten Commandments and the Sermon on the Mount . . .'

We got no further. A conversation of even that duration is like a profound dialogue when you have a script to finish, and the cameras are waiting, and a dozen facts to check, and producers and editors and production assistants criss-crossing their highly charged way through muddled compartments; and somebody like David Vine probably strode past saying, 'Gerry, we'd better get cracking.'

So I never did get a chance to develop that probe beneath the surface of things, but I have thought many times since that I would like to have replied that for most of my life I would have answered that question in almost exactly the same way.

I believe, what's more, that though the world has it's atheists (who have thought through the meaning of life and the claims of the Christian church and sincerely found them unacceptable), and its agnostics (who, likewise, have seriously considered the options and as yet not been able with conviction to come down on either side), and its legion of people who, out of laziness or weakness or in sheer preoccupation with the pleasure of the moment, really have not stopped to think at all – though the world is obviously made up of all these kinds, there is a vast population out there for whom the Christian faith means, more or less, what that famous sportsman said that day at Wimbledon.

They are decent, law-abiding and caring. They don't beat their wives, and they bring up their children to say 'God bless Mummy and Daddy' before they are tucked in for the night, and perhaps even have them Christened and take them to church.

They are people who respect standards and apply them to their own lives. They are wholly admirable.

What follows, I suppose, is written to my celebrity friend.

It is an attempt to say what I wanted to say that hurried evening but didn't have time. It is no more, and no less, than a description of how I (who would have claimed to belong to that great mass of people trying not to do the other chap down) came to learn what the Americans call *a whole new ball game*.

1: *A profile of ordinariness*

To understand, you may have to know something of the background: a sketch, no more, because our twig of the giant Williams tree is remarkable only for its ordinariness.

Mongrels, we are: Mother from Broad Norfolk stock, as far east as you can go across the flat acres just south of Cromer and its crab teas; Father from among the small dairy farmers in what used to be called Carmarthenshire before it was expanded into Dyfed, where cows trudge stoically over the hills through the mud, and men sing hymns with *hywl* in the village pubs.

To broaden our base still further, we three brothers (David, then me, then Mervyn) were reared, in the main, near the big houses of Upper Norwood, in South London, where the best people (not us) kept maids and Pekinese dogs and subscribed to the Conservative Party, but these days is a cosmopolitan dormitory that could do with a coat of paint.

The next thing you need to know is that our back garden, so far as middle son Gerald was concerned, at least, was notable for two features. One was that it backed on to some tennis courts, where, in successive generations, first that gentle Christian 'Bunny' Austin, then C M Jones, and later Roger Becker started their climb towards Davis Cup selection.

The other was that it was possible from our garden to guess the score at Selhurst Park on a Saturday afternoon, because you could hear the roar when Crystal Palace scored, and the groan when they conceded a goal.

They were potent influences on a boy for whom a firm volley into the chrysanthemums was the winning goal at Wembley, acclaimed with an exhalation of breath made to sound like the swell of eighty thousand voices, and the tennis ball that turned from the off and struck the dustbin was Miller's wicket down, and good riddance.

('Gerald, look what you're doing to your father's lawn! Now come on in and get on with your homework, there's a good boy.' I can hear it now.)

The footballers of Crystal Palace were nothing less than my first heroes, from the day I was first lifted over the turnstiles to see Tootill, Hudgell and Dawes, and all those other utterly unapproachable idols of mine. They were so God-like in their fame that once, I remember, being taken as an evacuee to Elm Park, because Palace were the visitors against Reading that afternoon, and I stood with my friend pressed up against the railings alongside the pitch in the breathless hope that I might be able to say a word to one of the men from far-off home in white shirts and black shorts.

Sure enough, that chance came. A player called Wilson took a throw-in just an arm's length in front of me, and I said a whispered soprano: 'Good luck, Wilson!' It was one of my earliest, and most mortifying, feelings of rejection that he didn't seem to hear me!

What on earth, by the way, would I have said in those days of short trousers and gas mask in a brown box if anyone had told me that one day I would actually get to know immortals like Stanley Matthews, and have them call me by my Christian name? It would have been too much. Yet befriend them I did, glory be! Maurice Edelston, who played for Reading in that match at Elm Park, was to be my colleague and friend and tandem commentator at Wimbledon before his early death; and the most buccaneering saint of all in my schooldays, Denis Compton, was years later to show to me one of the most simple acts of kindness I have known. To this day he does not know how much his telephone call helped when the world was falling to pieces round me.

So, you see, my gods were the cricketers and footballers of England. Whatever it was I did half a mile or so up the hill from our home in the big red-brick church of St John the Evangelist, *it*, surely, wasn't what you would call worship. The place, to this small boy, was a kind of cathedral theatre, where you talked in whispers, and Dad read the Lessons dressed in priestly robes, and Mother sat with her whist drive friends in an unobtrusive middle row, not entirely at ease at the bowing and the genuflecting, the plainsong and the chanting, but dutifully submissive, bless her big heart.

In this awesome place, in time, they dressed me up in robes you tripped on, and like some uncertain cherub I was processed alongside the tall man who swung the incense, nudged to go left, tugged to go right, elbowed to kneel, shoved to exit left, looking to see if Mum was watching and forgetting to stoke up with more incense from my shiny silver boat.

I progressed from that menial duty to the choir stalls, which meant being tossed into the stinging nettles as initiation, pretending by mime I was beginning to learn Stanford in E, and carving my initials on the stalls where big brother David had carved DJW before me.

Many times, since then, I have tried to analyse what effect it all had on me as I graduated into long trousers and then, after picking up bits and pieces of learning at umpteen schools, finally took my exams at the Queen

Elizabeth Grammar School in Carmarthen as we constantly flipped from the war zone of London to the countryside of Berkshire and West Wales.

In those confusing times, I think, was seeded the beginning of my spiritual schizophrenia, because I became familiar with two extremes of 'going to church on Sunday'. There was St John's, and the priests in their robes . . . and there was Aunty Maggie.

It was Aunty Maggie who first asked me if I was saved. And I didn't really know what she was talking about.

Aunty Maggie and Uncle Tom lived in an unpretentious terraced house in the climbing back streets of Carmarthen, and even as a boy I could tell she wasn't exactly *into* incense. She was *into* 'Thou Shalt not . . .' on the walls, as Dylan Thomas, from a few hills away, would have put it. 'Christ is the head of this house. The unseen guest at every table,' was pronounced from another vantage point in her tiny, polished kitchen.

She was a raw-boned lady in spotless apron, and I seem to remember her grey hair was done in a bun. She seemed endlessly to be making Welsh cakes, and endlessly cheerful; while Uncle Tom stroked the cat on his lap and quietly said 'Yes, indeed.'

In periods when we were shunted to Carmarthenshire for safety, Auntie Maggie and Uncle Tom would take me on Sundays to a little tumbledown mission hall in a winding street, where the people sang awfully loudly and talked in Welsh most of the time, though I could get the gist of it. And sometimes she would ask them if I could read a passage from the Bible, and I had to walk up front and do that in my strange accent.

It must have been a sharp culture shock, if nothing else. You see, the only people who read the Bible in St John's were the priests, or Dad, who was a lay-reader. And even they didn't just get up and read it like that:

there was all sorts of paraphernalia before they began to read.

Through those few years, anyway, Auntie Maggie kept asking me if I had been saved, and I kept eating her Welsh cakes. Now she's in heaven, making them Welsh cakes there, I hope she will be pleased to know that some (at the time) indefinable quality she possessed touched me more deeply than her repeated inquisition concerning my salvation.

That quality was most clearly demonstrated by her treatment of a celebrated town drunk who, in his more lucid moments, unshaven and scratching and malodorous, would call at her front door and mumble what she took to be a request for food.

'William Henry!' she would address him grandly in that shrill voice of hers that carried through from the narrow, fern-potted hallway, 'William Henry, come straight to the scullery and wash your hands, and you shall have some Welsh cakes fresh from the oven.'

And he would sit there, me backing off, and he would dribble and gorge, and Auntie Maggie would watch him with eyes aglow. Then, the feast devoured, she would send him packing, with a reminder to be at the mission hall on Sunday, and not to touch one drop – 'not one drop, mind!' – before he came.

I don't remember any tramps at St John's.

By eighteen, then, I was in mild rebellion over going to church on Sundays. I had started my first job by then, as a junior reporter on The Croydon Advertiser, and I was covering the Palace on Saturdays, and Mark Hart and Albert Finch when they boxed, and a young bank clerk from across the High Street, whose name was Gordon Pirie, seemed to be engaging my attention in those heady days.

There was, however, one tiny chink of light one day,

and it has only been in more recent years that I have fully recognised it.

I caught pneumonia. I had been quite ill at home. My first editor called, a gentle, dandruffed poet of a man, and he told my Mother I had been overworking in my enthusiasm for the job. Another day, one of the clergy called from our church, and my Mother came upstairs to announce that 'Father Martin' was here to see me. The reception I most probably gave this young priest was no doubt less than cordial: it wasn't just that I felt unwell, but priestly tones were by now altogether another world from the one I was discovering, the world of printing ink and magistrates' courts, by-lines and score-lines.

That was living: not Stanford in E.

But Fr Kenneth Martin persisted that day with the sullen young man in the bed, and before he left he took a snapshot from his wallet and handed it to me.

'Recognise anyone?' he asked.

It was a boxer in shorts and vest and traditional pose, hands up and gloved. It was obviously him.

And it was a first glimpse, no more, into the possibility that the religious world could be the same as the world of the sporting star. Years and years later, I looked up Fr Kenneth Martin in Crockford's, found an address and wrote to tell him how that incident had slept in the nooks and crannies of this boy's mind.

And how, twenty years later, this same surly boy helped modestly in the formation of 'Christians in Sport' in Britain because I had become certain they were not two worlds apart but the same.

He was thrilled to bits.

Since I have started to write this, something almost forgotten has surfaced vividly in my memory, and I recall it without comment because something urges me to do so.

That bout of pneumonia left me weakened. No more playing football for a year (I was left-back and kept my place because I arranged the matches), and no more tennis, either. Subsequently I was found to have a tubercular infection in a gland in my neck, which meant a course of injections, and an untimely interruption to my irresistible surge towards Fleet Street, and a by-line on the sports pages of a national newspaper. That was simply everything I wanted.

Somebody – I don't know who it was, but presumably one of my parents – arranged for me to see the vicar of a neighbouring church, All Saints, one weekday morning during this period of recuperation. I seem to remember it was explained to me that the Book of Common Prayer included a service for the healing of the sick. I would have gone along impelled by what, I wonder? Perhaps on the basis that anything was worth trying, because I was a young man in a hurry.

John White, the vicar of All Saints, had me kneel at the altar rail, the two of us completely alone in that place, and I remember that he lay hands on my head, rather the way the bishop had done at my confirmation at Swallowfield Parish Church, in Berkshire, several years earlier.

My state of health at that time was such that the only way I could take out an insurance policy on my life was by having it 'loaded'. It did not bother me in the least, but apparently I was not a very good bet to make even middle-age bones.

The point I make without comment is that I have never subsequently had any illness at all of that kind. I was soon back on the Sunday football field, and back on the tennis court hitting smashes (mainly off the wood) until it was too dark to see. There was never, at that time, a more persistent, or utterly artless, footballer or tennis player. Enthusiasm was my only merit; and I shouted a great deal.

My little skirmish with ill-health had one most helpful effect: it meant that I failed my medical for National Service. So while other young journalists of my generation were being honed at such exotic spas as Catterick, I was off following the star of my choice: to the Leicester Mercury (where they taught me well but didn't pay much), then to the South Wales Echo in Cardiff (where they tried to teach me the art of sub-editing, for which I had no skill and towards which I had no inclination.)

When The Croydon Advertiser invited me back, still in my early twenties, to be sports editor of their whole group of newspapers, I was on the next train to Paddington. The plan was to use that as a quick springboard to Fleet Street.

I never questioned my ability to get there, which was odd, because this confidence did not extend to other areas of my personality, though I was learning to develop a thin camouflage of the fact, a sort of swagger designed to hide the self-consciousness an occasional adolescent blush would betray. It also tended to bluff the imperceptive, so that they did not quickly spot the soft centre.

Fleet Street took an uncommonly long time to detect this rare talent in the southern suburbs, and even when the call finally came some nine or ten years later, it was not because the sports editor of the Daily Mail catapulted out of his seat, his green eye-shade flipping from his lid, and his cigar being prematurely stubbed because he had found a new Damon Runyan on the back page of the Advertiser he had picked up on the train from Caterham, but because he had idly said to his boxing writer, Harry Carpenter, one day:

'You don't know any young sub. we could take on, do you, by any chance?'

And Harry, by any chance, being at that time an

occasional reader of his local paper, said there was a lad called Williams in Croydon.

So much for romantic fantasies of the moment of discovery.

Fame, in that following year in the Street of Adventure and Other Hackneyed Phrases, was checking the greyhound results from far-away places like Hampton Wick, or sometimes vainly trying to nose out a split infinitive in Roy McKelvie's tennis prose from the Foro Italico, in Rome, and the grand-sounding Stade Roland Garros, in Paris.

A nation's tragedy provided me with my real opportunity. Eric Thompson, a sports writer and witty cartoonist from the Mail's Manchester office, was one of the people killed when the Manchester United football team's plane crashed in the slush at Munich Airport. Within a few weeks, because I had one car, no wife, intense ambition and an infuriating unwillingness to be chained to a desk when the sporting life was out there happening in the world, I was despatched north to Manchester.

It meant Crewe Alexandra on cold Tuesday nights, and Rochdale on perishing Saturdays; but, oh, it meant Old Trafford, too; and Anfield; and Bill Shankly at Huddersfield; and Bolton Wanderers, with big, amiable John Higgins, getting to the Cup Final at Wembley; it was Blackburn Rovers when they had Ronnie Clayton and Mike England and Bryan Douglas, and they really were a football team.

It meant scooping the Herald and the Express, and, sometimes, as a bonus, it meant being sent to the tennis when Roy McKelvie was away on weightier tournaments.

Covering the tennis took me to two people who changed the course of my life.

One was a pert and pretty little Scots girl who had to make up her mind, my news editor explained, whether

19

to become a tennis player or a singer. 'Good little story,' he said. 'They want a piece up in Scotland.'

The Scots girl was playing a tournament at Queen's Club in bed-sitterland, West Ken., where the ancient corridors have a certain Arctic charm. A few years later, though she was several years younger than me and there was parental concern over that, I married her.

I remember they sang 'Praise Him. Praise Him', and we were so nervous, one of us got the words wrong.

The tennis also, one summer's day, took me to the Northern club in Manchester, a few years later. At the time, it seemed of no importance at all, but a young British player, in a match I was idly watching, peppered the Didsbury sky with appeals to God.

'Jesus Christ!' he would scream when he missed a shot, which was not infrequent. I suppose I did not like it very much. My own limited but much-used vocabulary of swear words did not include that kind of profanity very often, I think, though merely out of some unrecognised instinct, not as a matter of careful self-discipline.

I walked away from that match because it was of no particular significance, and when the British player, crimson and scowling and defeated, walked furiously from the court towards the clubhouse half-an-hour later, untidily clutching towel and rackets, I happened to be within earshot as a burly, young man in open-necked shirt stood smiling in his path and said something like this to him:

'You know, you may not yet know Christ personally, but some people watching you possibly do. Can't you understand how we feel to hear you use His name like that?'

The tennis player would have hit him, except that the fellow in his path was built like a cross between a Rugby League player and an all-in wrestler. And perhaps because he did not have the merest trace of anger or

20

dislike in his face. He was smiling as if what he was saying was something quite different.

My reporter's instinct flashed alert signals then, and again a few hours later, in the fading light of the early evening, when I was taking a last precautionary meander round the courts before calling it a day. I had telephoned my story (which did not, by the way, include any mention of the incident that so intrigued me), so I was very much off-duty now, if such a condition exists in the journalist's life.

I should mention that I had vaguely been aware that, over the public address system, Spike had made an appeal for volunteer umpires to take charge of some mixed doubles matches that had to be completed that evening. Anyway, as I did my final tour of the tiny dramas of the day, I noticed that the British player who had earlier been appealing for Divine intervention (or perhaps cursing it) was now perspiring through a mixed doubles.

And sitting in the umpire's chair, dispensing justice, was the stocky young man who had so extraordinarily confronted him just a few hours before.

So I dallied in the bar that evening until the volunteer umpire who spoke for God was laughing with another man over a pint of orange squash. I introduced myself.

He said his name was Alan Godson. I was left to deduce that that most apt of names carried a 'reverend' in front of it, and I was to find out from others that he had played Rugby football with buccaneering unorthodoxy for Cambridge University and Lancashire.

He told me he was helping to run a sort of coffee bar in the centre of Manchester, The Catacombs, and he asked me if I was a Christian. I probably answered 'C of E', which was what I always wrote on forms. He took my address, and he soon began to send me paperbacks through the post.

I don't think I ever read them. I was too busy assembling a career, and relishing a marriage that was my paradise.

Besides, I was wary of religious fanatics.

2: *A slender thread*

Through those exciting, striving years, a slender thread held me to churchy things. In Manchester, I used to walk a hundred yards along the road from my homely lodgings to Poynton Parish Church. In Cardiff, I irregularly went to St John's, near the Western Mail offices. Then there was a church on a hill in Kenley, where I sometimes went on my own, and sometimes with my wife.

Fellowship never, though, progressed beyond a smile and a handshake at the door after the service. 'Nice to see you here again.' So it was very much a matter of Sunday churchgoing, then the real world on Monday.

My only reading was the newspapers. I had a black Bible (St James version, small print, two columns per flimsy page), on the fly leaf of which my Mother had written: 'Nahum 1: 7 – The Lord is good, a strong hold in the day of trouble'. It was the first word of prophesy I ever encountered, though I certainly did not recognise it as such for years and years.

I never read the Bible, though, and I never heard it read in church, except the Lessons, which I seldom understood, anyway.

What on earth was the influence that kept me from slipping completely away? Today I can recognise it, I think, as God honouring my parents' and Godparents' promises that day, a bawling, dripping infant, I was christened in St John's, alongside another noisy bundle of life who was never once to stray from the narrow path, and had a clerical collar on him in double quick time, without, mercifully, ever losing his sense of the ridiculous.

(Thank you, Ian, though I seldom see you now.)

Perhaps, too, it was God upholding me, however tenuously, for the shallow promise made at my confirmation. It had been a bit like, 'You, you and you. Two paces smartly forward and report for confirmation classes.' But we did sing, 'Oh, Jesus, I have promised to serve thee to the end . . .', and somewhere in that fourteen-year-old boy's mind there must have been some understanding of what it was about.

I fear it may have been no more than a pass to join the grown-ups at the altar rail when it was the Communion service.

That slender thread held, though, through the years when the Daily Mail brought me back to London, and afterwards, when Roy McKelvie left for the Sunday Express, made me their tennis correspondent. In far-off places, come Sunday morning, I would often find my way to a church.

There was a feeling of security, I suppose, a sense that we had not been completely taken over by the irresistible momentum of events. So I would scurry like some anonymous ant beneath the skyscrapers of Park Avenue, Manhattan, to be still for half an hour with a dozen other hushed worshippers in St Bartholemew's, everything polished till it glowed, and listen to an Ivy League American voice intone familiar words like, 'We do not presume to come to this Thy table. . .'

What, though, really are the motives of social churchgoing?

Is it some sentimental habit that lingers from cushioned days when parents were there to catch you when you fell? Is it some token recognition that there is a vague God out there, whom you don't mention on weekdays because, like politics, it only ends in acrimony? Is it nothing more than hedging your bets?

Or is it some half-answered call to an inner voice? Or is it all of these things?

And would it be more honest to abort this tedious pretence altogether, as many do, and settle for a God somewhere up there who knows you try to do your best in difficult circumstances and is going to play it fair when the time comes to settle the bill?

I hardly considered those things then, but I often do now. Then, I had no time for mystical thoughts. There were deadlines to meet, phone calls to make, planes to catch, words to find, grudges to feed, the famous to flatter, momentous sporting times to witness.

The job on the Mail was going well, and so was my wife's climb up the tennis ladder. I thought it was the perfect set-up: her name in the headlines, mine over the stories.

From Liverpool, where he had moved and was subsequently to become vicar of St Mary's, Edge Hill, on the borders of Toxteth, Alan Godson kept in touch, endlessly disturbing with his talk of God, and I wondered about the damage he was doing to my relationship with the tennis players when he would corner them at Wimbledon, and produce the inevitable paperback from his pocket.

Yet his commitment I begrudgingly admired. He seemed like Brighton Rock: if you break it in half, it says 'Brighton Rock' all the way through. Alan would say 'Jesus' all the way through.

The political slogan of the day was 'You've never had it so good,' and it certainly applied to me. If I had had my eyes open, I might have seen the warning signs sooner.

3: *The world came tumbling down*

Submerged deep inside me was a sense of fatalism, its origins I am only now beginning to recognise. In the short stories I tried to write, aping Somerset Maugham, they never finished up living happily ever after.

I make the point because Fleet Street eventually began to reveal its other face. It was not all 'Hold the front page' and 'Exclusive' over the banner headline. Even a week in Mexico City is spoiled by the key phone call to London that never gets through, or the cynical voice at the other end that refuses to see you have the greatest story ever told. You learn to miss shepherd's pie even in Paris.

Working for the Mail had its valleys as well as its mountain peaks, and after a few years, in my frustration, I began to consider opportunities that occurred in commercial television, and in the expanding industry of tennis.

The game had gone 'open' now, and there was a brave new world to be explored. With friends like John Dewar and Bob Howe, Jimmy Hill and Derek Penman I helped set up an indoor tennis circuit round Britain. We called it the Dewar Cup, and it was a success. I also nursed a dream, after going with my elder brother, David, one day to the Royal Choral Society's carol concert at the Royal Albert Hall, to take tennis there one day; and we did.

These were pressurised times in my life, but I was secure in the knowledge that there were two indestructible elements in it: my family, and my marriage. Possibly it was because I was so sure of them that I did not care for them more sensitively. I knew they were there, immovable, so I could climb my hills, and fight my battles, and come home exhausted: comfort and understanding would be there.

Then, in a period of just five (or was it six?) years, it all fell to pieces. All except my career, that is: that somehow survived.

The first hammer blow was my mother's death. Till that awful day, one way or another our family had fought off all the slings and arrows. We were untouchable. Death occurred in other homes: not ours.

If I had not been so busy looking everywhere else, I might have known that her increasing breathlessness was the warning sign, but my wife and I drove down to Wales to see the rest of the family one weekend – they were all encamped there in the hills by now – and, though she was resting longer in bed, she was the same caring, never-give-up Mum. We drove back to London on the Sunday night, happy at the way the break had gone, and I phoned my mother from a Cotswold pub while we took a breather.

When we arrived home, and got into bed, the telephone rang. It was one o'clock in the morning, and her life was over.

Don't let's dally on this. It happens, sooner or later, in all families, and the grief is personal, and somehow you bear it together. We were all stunned: we three brothers, and especially Dad. Their marriage had survived two World Wars, and one period, in the first, when he was a prisoner in Germany, and she did not know whether he was dead or alive. She had been his fortress. She had listened to everybody's stories. She had played her bridge, and she had backed the Tories every inch of the way.

There was an emptiness in all our lives after that.

In that grey fog of time, too, I became aware that my wife's sunshine kept disappearing behind the clouds. First it would be for days, and then the periods of estrangement became longer. I did not know how to deal with it. I suppose I just hoped it would go away, and it would be summer again.

After a year or more of these fits and starts, new beginnings that did not last, the end came with awful suddenness. My wife had fallen in love with someone else, and she went away. It happens all the time: you can read it in the tabloids. After eight years, we had become a social statistic. And the thing I remember best of that bleak autumn day, looking out on to the garden from an empty kitchen, was the sight of a fox wandering across the lawn. It's funny how you recall things like that.

At the time, I felt only a sense of betrayal, and I thought the hurt, the rejection, would never go away. Only now can I see how the pretty young thing I married grew up, and what she had wanted I could not give her.

The number I dialled for help, while the angels of compassion next door, Helen and Werner, dispensed wisdom, truth and mousaka at any hour of the day or night, was not 999, or the Samaritans, but Alan Godson's in Liverpool.

We talked for ages. Two days later, aware of my need, he jumped into his little car and drove all the way down the motorway to spend a few hours with me. On his return, he wrote to me:

'There is nothing in all creation that will ever be able to separate us from the love of God, which is ours through Christ Jesus our Lord' (Romans 8:39).

That, though, was Alan's conviction, deep in his heart. To me, at the time, it was incomprehensible even intellectually. It did not lessen the sense of desolation.

I prayed in the night to my vague God up there. I prayed for the ability to forgive: I had never been much good at forgiving, even minor trespasses. This was quite beyond me, but I kept asking, in anguish. The answer came two years later, when I had long given up. It came when I was not even thinking. One day I looked up, and it was as if the sun had melted the cloud, the way it does on a morning hilltop. I hoped she had forgiven me, too.

It was a miracle.

My rehabilitation was aided by good family, good friends and interesting work. My churchgoing became regular again: I was essentially an eight o'clock Communion man, because I valued the sacraments, liked the stillness; and, besides, it left me free for the garden and the housekeeping the rest of my day off. Gradually, over two or three years, the old confidence returned, and I began to back my own judgement again, judgements usually made on my emotional feelings.

After, I think, four years, I married again – suddenly, irrationally, passionately, seeking no guidance, giving time no chance, ignoring the storm clouds that hovered. The unwilling victim of my impetuosity did not seem certain whether to protest or take a chance with this reckless adventurer.

The song had promised that 'love is better the second time around', and I promised that it would be, for both of us. Besides, God would make it work this time. I took my gamble to Him, and asked, 'Please make it work this time.'

He didn't.

In days the thunder rumbled. In weeks the lightning flashed. In months we were apart. In two more years, as before, I reluctantly agreed to go through with a divorce. My head was like a beehive, buzzing with unanswered questions. How? Why? The hot-line to Liverpool grew hotter. I was like a fly at a light bulb looking for help. There were so many things I did not understand.

And in the middle of this new dilemma, my elder brother, David, who had wanted to be an Anglican priest and had for years expended energy he did not possess on helping the elderly and infirm, looked out over the Pembroke coast at Lydstep Haven one Sunday lunch-time, remarked to Dad on the beauty of the scene, and in minutes was on his way to heaven to help Mum with the Telegraph crossword.

Just a few minutes beforehand, he had posted me a card. On it, David wrote: 'Just enjoyed a lovely lunch. Now looking forward to an afternoon of relaxation.' The postcard arrived a couple of days later.

No more asthma now, Dai.

4: *Christians in sport*

Somewhere in all this I met up with some Christians in sport. One steamy day in Dallas, on Lamar and Norma Hunt's manicured lawns that slope down to lily ponds, as the famous and the wealthy, and those, like me, who got taken along for the ride, sipped our cocktails, I infiltrated a small group where Stan Smith was the obvious attraction.

Stan introduced me to his little American friend, Eddie, and, looking back now, I can see how that was crucial.

Eddie Waxer is his name, and he explained that he spent his life travelling the world ministering to professional sportsmen, or, broader than that, to sportsmen on the international scene. I told him about Alan Godson, and we agreed they should meet when Eddie came with Stan to Wimbledon in the summer. That meeting, in the busy walkway between the Centre and No 1 court, was to have great impact.

Alan dubbed him 'Waxbold', just as I had become his 'Jeremiah.' He never calls me anything else.

Eddie Waxer was also in touch with the De Gloria Trust, in Bromley, and with Ken Frampton's pretty assistant, Caryl, they convened a lunch in a Victoria hotel, to which several British Christians with sporting interests were invited. I was one of them: Alan Godson was another. We both went along.

Eddie had a vision. It was to extend the fellowship of Christian sportsmen to Britain. The main emphasis of that fellowship would be spiritually to reach well-known sportsmen and sportswomen, because they would have the greatest influence as they were encouraged to discipleship. It was important, he was convinced, that the ministry would take place, wherever possible, through men in the pastorate and working in church relationships.

He believed it was important for the church itself to gain the strength of new membership directly, and for the pastors to be influenced by ministering to players.

He cautioned that no attempt should be made to build a large structure of any kind, or that what was important 'was to become part of an organisation that called itself Christian.' There should be no hurry. With emphasis, he warned that the ministry should not be under pressure to produce for the general Christian public Christian witness of celebrity athletes, 'and thus destroy their lives in Christ.'

Eddie had faith that Great Britain would in time be the most significant country in the world for the sending of athletes who know Christ to other nations.

Some time later, Eddie arranged for a group of us from Britain to be guests for a week at a large, modern hotel in Orlando, Florida, where over one hundred and fifty professional sportsmen from America, with their wives, were holding an annual get-together. Most of the men were footballers: not Soccer players but American grid-iron footballers, not one of them under six feet two or less than fifteen stone! Giant, handsome sporting superstars, many of them. Men who had most of what the world has to offer. What set them apart was that they were all Christians, and what shamed me most was that they all knew their Bible.

Our little party from England included an athlete, hockey player and tennis player from Oxford University, Helen Bayley; Alan Godson, former Cambridge Rugby Blue; Harry Hughes, big, cheery centre half who used to play for West Bromwich Albion, Southport, Chelsea, Bournemouth and Gillingham, and now runs the Tottenham Hotspur shop; John Kilford, former Leeds United and Notts County full back, at that time a curate in Kent; the England international Rugby player, Peter Warfield; and the Oxford University seam bowler, Andrew Wingfield-Digby, since ordained in the Church of England.

The non-combatants among us included a Baptist minister from Farnborough, in Hampshire, Mike Pusey. Mike was already chaplain to Aldershot Football Club (which struck me as a task that required a good deal of faith). Mike was eager to see chaplains appointed at all Football League clubs in time.

Daily, starting at breakfast in a huge dining hall filled with large, round tables, we received Bible teaching from eminent men in the church in America. We were also split into small groups, according to our need, for more individual help. For myself, it was the first time in my life I had been exposed to Christian instruction of that sort, and had I been in a position of mental peace I would have benefited even more than I did.

There was also a great deal of boisterous fun that week, not all of it confined to the playing fields. Once, for instance, some of us were being tutored in the experience of introducing the topic of our faith in every-day situations, and I was paired off with Andrew Wingfield-Digby, a pocket booklet of 'The Four Spiritual Laws' in my hand, to practise an imaginary 'sell' on my next-door neighbour.

Andrew sat there trying to look serious as I said:

'Your lawn mower seems to be troubling you. Can I help at all?'

He was biting his cheeks now to conceal the smirk.

'You can't get it started, eh?' I persisted, self consciously. Then, accelerating sharply to the point: 'That's what happens when you have no power, you know. Now, have you read the Four Spiritual Laws, I wonder?'

Andrew was convulsed by now, and I hoped that God had a sense of humour.

Not all of it was to my taste, or what I had expected, but there were times of deeply moving reality as relationships were bared to each other, and experiences were shared.

I will never forget the morning a huge, black footballer was invited up to the microphone at one of the breakfast seminars to tell of a visit he had made the previous day, with some other footballers, to a local prison. He had no gift for public speaking. No verbal trick. No gloss. His very inability smoothly to articulate made his story the more compelling.

He got to the point where he was telling us how the prison chaplain had taken him into the cell of the hardest criminal in the jail, and how the man sat on his bunk, and would not even look up. And that mountain of a man, who would have known no physical fear on a football field, could not hold back the tears.

The dining room was gripped with silence.

Eventually, he said through his weeping, he had given up, and gone to another cell. Then, later, the chaplain said the prisoner in that first cell wanted him to go back again, and the big, black, craggy football star described how he had knelt on the stone floor with the hardest heart of them all, and the two men had prayed together.

You see things like that in films, or read of them in novels, and you get a sentimental glow, but you know it never happens like that in real life. This was real life, and there was something here for me.

Towards the end of the week, something was rankling me. Most of the sportsmen there in Orlando talked freely of the day when they had 'given their lives to the Lord', but I could not do that. I considered myself a Christian. What else had my Christening and my confirmation been about? I had become a sidesman at our local parish church at home.

However, if there was something I had to do to be absolutely certain, some positive act to resolve my confusion, I was prepared to make that formal request. One evening, before we left Orlando, two or three of us knelt in my room, and, hesitantly, I asked Jesus to enter my life, so that I could be certain it happened there, that day. Aptly, I remember, Alan was kneeling right alongside me in support.

It had been a disturbing, encouraging week. Deep feelings had been touched, and some cherished traditions questioned. We climbed into our Jumbo feeling that God could do something through Christians in Sport in Britain if we made ourselves available. Above all, I think, we felt tired.

The Godson man, never! He wanted to evangelise the whole plane. I wanted to sleep, and sleep I did, fitfully. Once, when I awoke in my cramped discomfort, I noticed Alan deep in conversation with an air hostess in the back seat.

5: *Awake, sleeper!*

Everybody's looking for the same thing, only some call it happiness, some call it joy, others say peace. But we all want it, deep down.

We look for it in different places. One man thinks he will find fulfilment in riches: a Rolls in the drive, a chalet in St Tropez, an office in Mayfair, a manor in Sussex.

To another, the spur is fame: to be flattered and courted, to be pictured in the papers and on the television screen. To one man, the quest for knowledge brings life. To another the search is for the freedom to 'do his own thing', for a mountain-side away from the jungle of competition.

Or happiness is in none of these places. We look for it in a bottle, in pills and syringe till the habits absorb us, and we try to turn away but can't. Or the answer may be found in power and position, we think.

But the nursing homes, the bars and the graveyards are full of the disillusioned and the cheated.

We sense a call to spiritual things, but our culture has so many gods. We climb Katmandu. We bow to our gurus. We join cults and communes. Even the Christians speak in conflicting tones. It is so confusing. Why bother?

Then, one day, you get to the very end. Either God

exists, or He does not. There is a decision to be made, and the dying man has no time to listen to religious men debate their liturgy and dogma. You need proof in that place where you begin and end, in your heart. And it is desperately urgent.

God, surely, has to be greater than dry doctrine, or the superstition of statues and lighted candles; greater than the emotion of the evangelist's packed arena. He has to be more than vestments and panoply, more than black Bibles and grey formalism. More than rhetoric. More than recitation. More than hymns and PCCs and elders and summer fetes.

He has to be more than standing up and kneeling down, and turn to page 13 in Series 3. More than raising arms in the air and clapping hands and bringing in the guitars.

If God is only a God of history, if Jesus was a good and wise prophet who lived two thousand years ago, and said 'Do this', and that's all, you might as well give up the quest, live for the day, and accept that eventually there will be no more days. And that's it.

One day, drained and buffeted amid the ruins of my second marriage, I got to that point, and in the dead of night, alone in my house, I raged at God in anguish: 'Prove yourself!' Looking back, I can see it was the turning point, because at that moment it was just me, alone, and God, if he existed: the paraphernalia of religion consumed in the fire.

I don't know whether I expected to hear a voice or the crack of thunder, or see a vision or to be magically transported to another level of consciousness. I think, perhaps, I expected nothing; and nothing happened.

At least, nothing happened when I was looking. It began to happen when I was not even paying attention. I was driving back from Llangynog one day, back to the Beeb, to work, to the roses in Epsom, and, as always, I broke my journey a mile off the M4 in Newport, where a friend since footballing days, Keith Tyte, is a canon in the Church in Wales, and chaplain to Newport County Football Club, a sincere and trusted pal, an ordinary man with deep pastoral gifts, and a loyal Welsh wife, Gwen.

Through the years, we have loved our sport together, Keith and I, and laughed a lot, and abused referees from the stand as all good Soccermen do. He had been constant, and he had been there in the bad times, never with a glib text, but with a quality of friendship that is not easy to find.

We talked of many things, and I drank their coffee, and then I had to be on my way again. As I was leaving, Keith asked me:

'What are you reading? Look, I've been sent this. You might find it interesting.' He handed me a paperback, and to this day I don't know whether he had read it himself.

On the cover was a young, robed Anglican priest standing in front of an altar. The book was called *When the Spirit Comes*. It was by a man named Colin Urquhart. I had never heard of him.

He wrote something in his book that was so startling, and spoke so unerringly to my need, that I was exhilarated. He said that God was still alive and well.

It was like a bright dawning.

The book recounted how Colin Urquhart, a young Church of England clergyman in an unremarkable parish in the Home Counties, became aware of his need for something more in his life, and how he came into an altogether deeper understanding of God, and of God's power to change people and things HERE AND NOW. God answered him with a miracle of healing, and by transforming this man's ministry.

He did it by His power in the vast world beyond human

knowledge and understanding: in the supernatural. God did it by His Holy Spirit.

Now, the Holy Spirit was something I had unthinkingly consigned to the 'too difficult' tray of my life. I had only the vaguest notion of what the words meant. Through the years, I had heard clergymen say, at the end of a service, 'The grace of our Lord Jesus Christ, and the love of God, and the fellowship of The Holy Ghost, be with you all.' They had a comforting sound of peace and reassurance, but they were lifeless words.

I had also, countless times, stood in congregations and recited, in the creed, my belief in The Holy Ghost. But they were empty words.

What on earth – or in heaven, I suppose – was this Holy Ghost? It seemed to me that, as a child some time, I had imagined an ethereal figure in a white sheet, like Dad dressing up at party time, and decided it was all too spooky for me. Through all those subsequent years I had never heard even one sermon on the subject of The Holy Ghost; or, if I had, then I was not listening.

And here was this man Colin Urquhart calling it – Him – The Holy Spirit, and proclaiming that He was still active in the Eighties. It was astounding.

God alive! He could miraculously heal today, speak through men today. This was not a story about people who lived in a different and remote period of history. It was about today. It was about people who lived in semi-detached houses, and went to the office, and had mortgages to pay, and liked pop music, and wore denims, and played squash at the local leisure centre, and found the boss a pain in the neck, and got constipated.

If this was for real, this was for me. Something inside me was stirring. I began to talk to God almost as if I imagined He might hear me. I am not sure whether I thought he could answer me.

Then, one Sunday morning, I found myself with the

luxury of fifteen minutes to spare and nothing to do before I went off to church. I would pay some bills: you know, the electricity, the rates, the threatening buff envelopes that had waited, unopened, on the little coffee table where I keep writing pad and envelopes. I got out my cheque book, and I needed to know the date.

Now, there were four or five places I could have looked for the date that morning. There was my digital wrist watch: either of two diaries I used to keep, one for business engagements, one for social things: there was a calendar on the kitchen wall, and another one in the hallway.

By instinct – instinct? I went to one of the diaries. And scribbled in that very day was this entry: 'Colin Urquhart at St Paul's this evening.' I am not sure whether you actually do blink in disbelief, or whether it is just another cliché, but if you do, then I did.

I had no recollection whatever of ever having written those words. I did not think I had ever heard of Colin Urquhart until I read his book, 'When the Spirit Comes'. Yet I was not so far gone in the head to believe that God impersonates people's handwriting. Just for a moment, I think I must have recoiled at the thought of such strange goings-on.

Then, dimly, I remembered that months earlier, as I was leaving a Bible study at a doctor friend's house one evening, he had said, 'Oh, by the way, Colin Urquhart's speaking at St Paul's on such-and-such a date,' and, because I did not want to appear too ignorant to the learned and spiritual people present that evening, I resisted asking, 'Who's Colin Urquhart?', and quietly made a note in my diary.

Then I totally forgot about it. There were a few other things in my life to be getting on with.

I phoned my doctor friend excitedly. 'Gareth, is Colin Urquhart still speaking at your church this morning? He is. Is it all right if I come along with you and Mary to hear him? OK. Save me a seat. I'll be there.'

That morning, at St Paul's Church, Howell Hill, in Cheam, I sat riveted by what was said. It was a repeat of what he had written, of course, but with freshened insight. And it was not in a book this time: the man it happened to was there, in the flesh, in that small, modern church. The feeling inside me began to grow: there is truth here.

Alone, though, at home, lying in bed, an insidious voice inside me wanted to reason it out, sort the logic from the fantasy. Yes, it had been odd how I had just happened to go to that particular diary at that particular moment on this particular day, but coincidences do happen, don't they?

'Oh, Lord,' I seemed to say from within, 'if you're not kidding me, give me some proof.'

The very next morning, I reached the top of the escalator at Oxford Circus tube station on my way to Broadcasting House, and in the busy scrum of a London morning I bumped physically into Colin Urquhart. He was with his wife and, I seem to remember, a child. I muttered something about how much I had appreciated what he had said at St Paul's the morning before, and he seemed shy about it. And that was all.

He, I am sure, will not even remember it. To me, it was another sign, and they were pointing to a God who was real, who might actually be able to help me in my bewilderment, and take away that dull feeling of being left alone entirely to our own limited resources on a planet fast spinnimg out of control.

Yes, it was a sign, and more came thick and fast. I was eager to follow them, but I was not going to be deceived. This Holy Spirit business had to be real, or I wanted none of it.

One of the adjustments that had to be made in my

thinking was my attitude to the great unknown. Till now it had been one of slightly derisive but good humoured acceptance that 'somebody out there wanted to speak to somebody down here' as a small group of slightly odd and usually elderly people sat in a darkened, musty room seeking to communicate with dead aunts and uncles. You know, Margaret Rutherford's Madame Arcati in 'Blithe Spirit', a figure of fun, but some credibility, as well.

Things that went bump in the night, devils and demons and witchcraft, I had considered too far-fetched to bother with, but of the more reasonable areas beyond normal understanding – 'the stars foretell' in the newspapers, transcendental meditation, yoga, hypnotism, all that sort of stuff – I was tolerant without being particularly interested. (At the time, I had better add, I was far too unfamiliar with my Bible to know how categorically God denounces the occult.)

My acquaintance, then, with the supernatural was rather less than a nodding one. All the same, I never doubted that strange things did genuinely happen beyond our ken. It seemed arrogant to suggest that even the sum total of man's knowledge, at any moment in history, could but scratch the surface of ultimate truth.

The dilemma is to distinguish the real from the spurious. If you pick up an apple, you know you have an apple in your hand, but when it comes to the senses, to the intangible, then we are vulnerable to cranks and phonies and worse. Is that fear of being duped, though, good reason to abandon the search for knowledge while you still have two feet on the ground, two hands on the safety rail, and the seat belt strapped tightly round your waist?

I began to receive assurance from passages in that book I was starting to read more and more as my exploration hesitantly, but hungrily, began: passages like this one,

43

from Luke 11, verse 11: 'Would any of you who are fathers give your son a snake when he asks for fish? Or would you give him a scorpion when he asks for an egg?'

If there really is a God up there, I reasoned, and if He really is alive, surely He would be able to see in my heart that my search for Him was sincere. He would not give me a Hammer horror film to be getting on with.

There was this verse, too, that followed on immediately in Luke 11: 'How much more, then, will the Father in heaven give the Holy Spirit to those who ask him?'

It was a question of knowing how, and when and where to ask. But I was hot on the trail.

6: *Finding firm foundations*

'So then, anyone who hears these words of
mine and obeys them is like a wise man who
built his house on rock. The rain poured
down, the rivers overflowed, the wind blew
hard against that house. But it did not fall,
because it was built on rock.'

Matthew 7: 24–25

From somewhere in the nooks and crannies of the mind
came an insatiable hunger to read about the Christian
faith, to discover what it really did mean. The images of
understanding I possessed were such moving shadows
that I could barely articulate them. There was much to
un-learn, much, much more to learn.

What, though, should be my priority? Sanctification?
(I had not even known what it meant) Baptism in the
Spirit? Fullness? Salvation? Holiness? Already, I had
read enough to recognise that I was tiptoeing through
a linguistic minefield. The point was, I was reading:
devouring every Christian paperback I could find,
reading even the Bible.

Till then, it had not been much more than a black
cover on the bookshelf, or something I took along, carefully hidden while I walked from my car to the door,

when I was invited to a 'Bible study'. (How I dislike that label. It sounds so unexciting, so much a matter of discipline.)

My teacher came from within me. Passages from the Bible began to light up as I discovered them, and without trying to memorise them I found that I did. So what ought my priority to be at this first stage of my great exploration? Up jumped the verse (Psalm 37:4): 'Seek your happiness in the Lord, and He will give you your heart's desire.' And then (Matthew 6:33): 'Seek ye first the Kingdom of God, and all these things shall be added unto you.'

To discover the Kingdom of God, I reasoned, I first had to know exactly who God is; and the Bible told me that to know who God is, and what He is like, I had to know the person of Jesus. There was the key figure: this Jesus. He had said: 'If you knew me, you would know my Father also.' (John 8:19) And, 'Whoever has seen me has seen the Father' (John 14:9)

The Bible, I discovered, claimed; 'Christ is the visible likeness of the invisible God' (Col 1:15)

And: 'He . . . is the exact likeness of God's own being . . .' (Heb 1:3).

When, for the first time in my life, I seriously came to investigate the historical figure of Jesus Christ, why He came, who He was, how He lived, why He died, I came upon that word again. It was here that, before anything else, I had to clear, and then make up, my mind.

The supernatural.

I could see now, with shining clarity, that central to the whole story of Jesus, His miracles, His resurrection, and the sending of His Holy Spirit, was this fundamental question: could I believe, did I believe, that Christ came back from the dead?

Paul summed it up like this, in 1 Corinthians 15:14:

'If Christ has not been raised from death, then we have nothing to preach and you have nothing to believe.' So there was no mystical jiggery-pokery from Paul: here he was admitting that the whole Christian case rested on this point.

In fact, in his letter to the Romans (Chapter 10, 9–10) Paul sets it out starkly as an essential tenet of belief: 'If you confess that Jesus is Lord, *and believe that God raised Him from death*, you will be saved.'

So: was God capable of a supernatural act so enormous that He could overcome this ultimate? DEATH. Well, was He? All my life I had swept the resurrection under the carpet. If anyone had asked me about it, I would have spiritualised it; but, then, why should anyone have asked me in the first place? My 'religion' had been a private matter to me.

I suppose that is why a vivid and moving musical like 'Jesus Christ Superstar' avoided the problem of presenting the resurrection at the end. It was simpler to have a motor coach disappearing into the dust of the desert. But the Bible does not let the true seeker get away with evasiveness.

It does not allow him to believe what he likes. The edges cannot be blurred.

The Bible says that, after His crucifixion and death at Calvary, Jesus suddenly stood among His disciples and said: 'Look at my hands and my feet, and see that it is I myself. Feel me, and you will know, for a ghost doesn't have flesh and bones, as you can see I have.' (Luke 24:39)

Luke goes on to report that Jesus showed them His hands and His feet, but they still could not believe, they were so full of joy and wonder; so Luke says that Jesus asked them: 'Have you anything here to eat?' They gave Him a piece of cooked fish 'which He took and ate in their presence.' (verse 43).

That momentous fish supper was not the only evidence, either. In 1 Corinthians 15(5–7) Paul testifies: 'He appeared to Peter and then to all twelve apostles. Then He appeared to more than five hundred of His followers at once . . .' Spiritualise that!

Now, of course, you may scoff and say that the Bible is not to be taken literally, that it has been translated and distorted through the ages. Many people do say that. I know that I did. By now, though, I was coming to this conclusion: that for the Bible to have remained the best-seller of all time when tyrants and intellectuals have sought to ridicule and disprove it, even to ban it, and people have suffered horrendous deaths by torture for daring to believe it, it must somehow have been protected by God.

God would not protect downright lies.

I still wrestled with the dilemma: how did God do it, though? How did he bring Jesus back from the dead? Then, one day in New York City, as I was browsing through some pamphlets in a church, I picked up a tiny booklet you could read in ten minutes. It was about the miracles, and it said this: that because God made the world, He made everything in it, including the natural laws, and therefore He was master of the natural laws.

In other words, because God created the force of gravity, He could alter it at His will. He could make a waterfall go up instead of down, except that He is not in the conjuring trick business. There was nothing God could not do, because He was the ultimate intelligence who created everything.

If He wanted to, God could quite simply bring His own son back from death. And Jesus, somehow being God, could likewise superimpose His will on the laws of nature. Hence His miracles. QED. Like a window of the mind being opened, it was suddenly daylight. How could it have been such a mystery to me all those years?

Here, being revealed to me, was the God who ruled even the supernatural.

My excitement mounted. Up jumped a verse from Ephesians 1. Paul wrote in verse 19: 'And how very great is His power at work in us who believe. This power working in us is the same as the mighty strength which He used when He raised Christ from death . . .' So it was all about power, not of intellectual investigation and logic, after all: on the contrary. I found that Paul had confirmed that in 1 Corinthians 4:20: 'For the Kingdom of God is not a matter of words but of power.'

It was very definitely not man's power, either. John 6:63 proclaimed: 'What gives life is God's Spirit; man's power is of no use at all.'

Somehow I had to understand what it meant to rely on this power: on the Holy Spirit. Of all places, I was given a lesson in Palm Springs, California. We were luxuriously coralled there for a week, covering a women's tennis tournament, feted and pampered among the palm trees and the tumbleweed, limousined down Frank Sinatra Drive to Rancho Mirage, pointed out Bob Hope's place up on the craggy hill. It was all a dreamland of self-indulgence. You did not want a social conscience to disturb your enjoyment.

I had taken a book about Katherine Kuhlman's extraordinary life of miraculous healing of the sick, done in Jesus' name. One of the many benefits of my job as BBC tennis correspondent was that there was plenty of reading time in trans-continental flights, and in hotel rooms before the matches began. The account of Miss Kuhlman's life was riveting: I could not put it down. I read it quickly once, then, more searchingly, again. It sharpened my sense that there was something I had to learn about letting loose, and letting God. I needed some illumination.

Every morning, during that week, the British tennis

writers would pull on their swimming trunks when they woke up and head straight for the hotel pool. By nine o'clock, the Californian sun was toasting hot, and we would lie under the palm trees till hostesses brought us our breakfast. Then, having barely digested it, we would jump into the pool.

I could swim, but I had never learned how to float. And I wanted to. But when I tried to imitate the husky, bronzed young men lying serenely on their backs in the water, I panicked – and disappeared, kicking and gurgling, beneath the surface.

I tried again – and submerged, all flailing distrust. And again – and this time a voice from the side of the pool, one of the tennis writers, called: 'Hey, Williams! You know, if you want to float, you've got to trust the water!'

Trust the water: its buoyancy. Believe – and really believe – that it could take my weight if I did not resist. One more try. Now trust the water.

I lay back, kept my bottom up, kept my legs up stiffly, let the warm water block up my ears . . . and I put the water to the test. It did not let me down. I floated. It was heaven. I just lay there on its gentle cushion, looking up at the blue sky, feeling the hot sun, bewitched by the silver of the San Jacinto mountains as they cascaded down to the back of the little town. All I had had to do was trust.

To my colleagues, laughing and cheering over their drinks, it was merely someone learning to float. To me, at that time of my life, it was a lesson infinitely more profound than that. I knew I had to learn really to believe in God, really to trust His Holy Spirit: not in words but in truth.

I had to learn faith, the analysis of which I had found in the first verse of Hebrews 11: 'To have faith is to be sure of the things we hope for, to be certain of the things we cannot see.' Now that's some faith!

I had not only to cultivate such faith (how on earth could I do that, anyway?) but to understand that the Bible says faith, not good deeds, is the essence of the Christian life. There it was crystallised in Romans 3: 22–26:

'God puts people right through their faith in Jesus Christ. God does this to all who believe in Christ, because there is no difference at all: everyone has sinned and is far away from God's saving presence. By the free gift of God's grace all are put right with Him through Christ Jesus, who sets them free.

'God offered Him, so that by His death He should become the means by which people's sins are forgiven through their faith in Him. God did this in order to demonstrate that He is righteous.'

Faith! More than courage! more than guts. Something implanted deep in the heart, supernaturally. The immovable conviction that made Noah willing to become one of the classic laughing stocks of history by building his boat, and taking in the animals, two by two. The quality that enabled Abraham, blindly almost, to leave his own home and venture to a country that he believed God had promised to give him. The impulse that prompted the woman with internal bleeding to be certain, somehow, that if she merely touched Jesus' clothes she would get well. She did get well, and Jesus told her, 'Your faith has made you well' (Mark 5:34).

Faith! The certainty of the heart that made Jairus, an official of the synagogue, ask Jesus to heal his daughter even though they had brought him the message that she had died. The story is in the same chapter.

The Bible is a catalogue of tales of people of faith: not of tepid, wavering sentiment, but absolute certainty. And subsequent history is full of stories of other men of this faith. The world abounds with them still today: men derided, slandered, imprisoned, murdered even.

Faith! This inestimable thing. This mystery.

The Bible, I discovered, said that the life of a Christian is all about it. 'For our life is a matter of faith, not of sight,' Paul wrote in 2 Corinthians 5:7.

Jesus himself put it even more dynamically. He said: 'Everything is possible for the person who has faith.' (Mark 9.23).

The problem was: how to get it.

All this was meaty stuff, and I needed time to ponder on it. If I could develop such faith somehow (and that would be a mountainous task, surely) it would have to be seen in action: often less, not more, action from me. I had to stop trying to do it all myself, and give God the credit for being capable of acting in any circumstance. I had to stop making decisions without careful thought and prayer, and without consulting wise Christian friends, and without seeing what the Bible had to say.

I would have to let the stress melt away. (Already I was learning from Oswald Chambers, in his daily readings *My Utmost For His Highest*, that to be anxious really meant: 'I don't trust you, Lord. You're going to let me down at the last moment! The challenge of that statement had bitten deeply into me.)

So I was coming to an appreciation of real faith, but I still lacked it. It was not, for example, that I did not believe all those incidents of divine healing in the book about Katherine Kuhlman's ministry, it was just that I needed proof! They were miracles recorded in a book about people I had never met, and never would meet. If only I could actually see one of these people with my own eyes.

On the flight back to London from Palm Springs, our small group of journalists was split up because there was a large and jolly party of middle-aged American husbands and wives on board. Two of them sat next to me, and because I was so engrossed in my book I did not get into conversation with them until the meal was served.

Then the lady spoke. 'I see you're reading about Katherine Kuhlman,' she said pleasantly. 'Are you a Christian, then, I wonder? We are. We're all from the same church, you know. On our way to Europe.'

We talked about the book, and I said how intrigued I was by the instances of healing that seemed to abound in the church today. But if only I could actually meet someone who had personally received a miracle of healing.

'Oh,' said the American lady. 'You must talk to our pastor's wife back there. She went to one of Katherine Kuhlman's meetings, and went forward for prayer, and she was healed of a cancer in her throat.'

It was a time of things happening like that. And things went on happening like that.

My obsession now was with the 'signs and wonders' that Jesus performed during his life on earth, which His early followers were also given the power to perform (just read the book of Acts!), and which Christians today were apparently repeating all over the world. How much easier to believe in a God who could still break through the perimeters of nature and demonstrate His presence and sovereignty today, than in some ineffectual figure fossilised and cobwebbed in the tomb of ancient history.

Canon Jim Glennon, an Australian, clarified things for me in his book, 'Your Healing is Within You', and Fr Francis MacNutt's 'Healing' seemed almost the ultimate Christian textbook on the subject. I read it two or three times to unravel some of the complexities that still baffled me.

The miracles of utterly transformed lives gripped me, as well, like the tales of boys and girls rescued from dereliction, from drug abuse and gang killings, rape and prostitution and worse in the slums of New York City by a skinny country pastor named David Wilkerson. I was thrilled by the God of 'The Cross and The Switchblade'. Never had I heard of God moving so dramatically in the real dirt of today.

Nobody told me what to read: that was the point. I somehow came upon all these books, and I do not even remember where. I read *They Speak in Other Tongues*, and *Nine O'clock in the Morning*. I read everything I could find by Michael Harper. David Watson's *One in the Spirit* was another Godsend – and I mean Godsend! – for its authenticity, its balance and its clearness. Next, I found another essential to my library: *I Believe in the Holy Spirit*, by Michael Green: scholarly, comprehensive and lucid.

My research was subtly shifting by now from miracles of healing to the source of this extraordinary power: I was back to the Holy Spirit, searching for what it meant, and how 'it' could be received with certainty. The same thorny phrase kept pricking me: 'the baptism of the Holy Spirit.' Clearly, things were coming up to a head, and three more books accelerated that sprint.

You see, what I wanted to know was this: were we given God's Spirit the moment we believed, and had we merely to believe it in faith? Or were we given His Spirit with certainty? After all, in John 14:21 Jesus promised: 'Whoever loves me, I too will love him and reveal myself to him.' The word 'reveal' carries the promise, surely, of something being made known in some recognisable way.

Now I found this, in Dr Martin Lloyd-Jones' book *Life in the Spirit*: 'It is important to keep these things clear. The 'baptism' with the Spirit, the 'sealing' of the Spirit, is a definite concrete experience. It is mainly concerned with the question of assurance and of certainty

– it is a very definite experience. It is not something that you 'receive by faith': a man knows whether he is sealed with the Spirit or not. One cannot be baptised with the Spirit without knowing it.'

That was emphatic. So was what I unearthed in Dr A W Tozer's *When He is Come*. Dr Tozer wrote this: 'I can be dogmatic about this on the basis of deep study: no-one was ever filled with the Holy Ghost who didn't know that he had been so filled!'

I was certain, then, that I had not been filled, or baptised, with the Holy Spirit, whether they were one and the same thing or not. At this crucial point I came upon a book that raised still more fundamental doubts in my mind.

The book was called, *Truth To Tell*.

7: *Truth to know*

My pal Harry Hughes rang me one day, about this time in my life, and asked: 'Would you like to come and talk about your job to the men's society at our church, Gerald?'

Unhesitatingly, I said: 'Yes, of course,' because Harry Hughes, the big, jokey former professional footballer who was in that original group of us who flew to Orlando and then returned to start 'Christians in Sport', is a tonic. He is a fresh sea breeze of a man, warm and boisterous and invigorating. I love being with him, with his wife, Joyce, and their family: they are my type of people. Open and unsubtle.

You don't have to work your way through veils of reserve and caution to get at the Hugheses: they're right there in the shop window, alive and normal, no pretence. These days they manage the Tottenham Hotspur Football Club shops, and through their work they engender a wealth of goodwill among the kids who support Spurs and swarm up against Harry's counters on match days to buy Tottenham favours.

Just about the only thing I knew about the church they belonged to in those days was that it was where they used to live: in Guildford. I did not know what banner it flew, or its name tag, and I did not care, either, because I had already developed a dislike of denominational barriers, and this conviction has grown.

I believe they are an offence to God, and a disastrous witness to the great world out there.

But I digress. This chapter is about what happened when I read 'Truth to Tell', though it was important that your first knew about Harry Hughes' invitation to his church men's society.

The cover of the little book tells it plainly. 'Truth to Tell' describes itself as 'an exposition of basic Christian truths', and its author is a man named David Pawson. It says something of where I had been all my church life (I hesitate to say 'Christian life') that I had not heard of him before.

Building his case like a lawyer, David Pawson at first considers the alternatives to the Christian view of life, and how it began, and then easily picks his way through the rudiments of the faith. I had never before seen the argument put so clearly, or so logically. His book is a plain man's guide to Jesus.

I was gripped by his simplicity, his avoidance of religious jargon, or of the history of doctrine, which no doubt has its value in the Christian library, but is confusing to the seeker hacking his puzzled way through the dense undergrowth left by generations of people more concerned with the form and practice of religious observance than the uncluttered truth of the story of Jesus.

Thank heaven (and I mean that!) that you do not have to be a university don or a student of divinity (both of which I should like to have been) to reach a point of intellectual belief in the Christ of the Bible. 'For God, in His wisdom, made it impossible for people to know Him by means of their own wisdom,' wrote Paul in 1 Corinthians 1.

It's just as well, or the likes of me would never make it.

It was in the second half of 'Truth to Tell' that I was hit hardest: a chapter headed: 'Got a conversion complex?' There, David Pawson emphasises that although, in one vital sense, it is an act of God that seals a person's conversion to the Christian faith, there is a part we humans have to play in it that is rather more complex than some people think.

There are, he claims, at least five elements in conversion.

The first, he lists, is repentance from sin. He writes:

'There is no half way in this process. It involves a willingness to be rid of every evil thing, however dear it is to us, and even some neutral things (like certain relationships, hobbies or pursuits) which, while harmless in themselves, have got between us and God. . . . Repentance is simply the willingness to turn, without condition.'

The second element, writes David, is faith towards Jesus: 'A total trust in Christ's competence to do what He has promised.'

The third element is baptism in water:

'Basically, baptism is two things, a burial and a bath. It is the disposal of the old life . . . and the starting clean with the new one, coming up out of the water into the new, risen life. Nothing could possibly represent more vividly than that what conversion is all about.'

And David, just before that, declares: 'If someone is converted but not baptised, we may correctly see the process of conversion as incomplete.'

Element number four, according to David Pawson, is filling with Holy Spirit:

'Being filled with Spirit, like baptism, is meant to be part of the process of conversion.'

And, finally, the fifth element is membership of a church:

'The New Testament knows nothing of Christians

who are, or at any rate remain, unrepentant, unbaptised, unfilled . . . or unchurched. It simply assumes that all those who believe in Christ are integrated into the local church under local leaders. . . .

'To leave out the body, the church, is to omit the corporate aspect and to imply that conversion is a highly individual, private matter. . . . We cannot separate the Head from the body.'

So wrote this man David Pawson, and suddenly I would have given anything to meet him, and talk to him, because his book, at notably this chapter, both disturbed and challenged, and, in another way, fuelled me. It made me ask questions about myself, about the scriptural truth of whatever Christian experience I had known.

For example, I had been christened as a baby, and when I bothered to think about it I felt comfortable that God would have honoured the sincere prayers of my parents and Godparents, simply because He always honours honest prayers. At least I had got that far in my understanding of Him.

But I had not been 'baptised in water', not the way David Pawson seemed to be talking about; and not the way, either (which became of growing importance to me) that Jesus himself was baptised (Luke 3:21; Matthew 3:13–17; Mark 1:9–11). In fact, in the second of those accounts Matthew records that Jesus said after His baptism: 'For in this way we shall do all that God requires.'

Now the more I considered it, I could not conceive that Joseph and Mary would not have offered their baby to God when he was born, and yet Christ, at his own moment of spiritual maturity, still elected to be baptised in the River Jordan.

I had subsequently been confirmed into the Church of England, but I had to own up to the truth that if that was a genuine time of commitment and infilling of the

Spirit, then there had been precious little evidence of it in the years that followed. I would have to say that my position now, having been baptised by total immersion in what we may call mid-life, is that I firmly believe it to be far more scriptural, and infinitely more vivid a moment, than my confirmation.

I have not been in the least bit surprised by the number of Anglicans whose search for a deeper walk with God has led them to the waters of baptism. I only wish the Anglican church (which I have never left) could open its heart to a reappraisal of the whole sequence of infant baptism and confirmation that might lead to a service of baptism by immersion at the point in one's life when a mature commitment can be made.

Anyway, the element among David Pawson's listed five that most concerned me at the time I read his book was the fourth: filling with the Holy Spirit.

Because of the events of my recent life, because I had to make decisions that concerned not merely my own spiritual wellbeing, I desperately needed the assurance that the Spirit of God lived in me. It was not something I could work up for myself. It was not something I could learn from reading. It was not an assurance that any well-meaning friend could give me.

'You have to accept by faith' didn't work. I needed to know, without doubt, in my heart. And somehow David Pawson had emerged as a man to lead me to that truth. How to meet him, that was the question.

The telephone rang. It always does in my house. It was Harry Hughes.

'Gerald, you haven't forgotten you're coming to speak at our church next Wednesday evening?'

'No, of course not.' (Quick squint in my diary to see the evening was clear.)

'We're looking forward to seeing you. Our pastor is,

especially,' said Harry, reassuringly. 'Once you've met him, you know, your life will never be the same again.'

'I could do with meeting someone like that, Harry! What's his name?'

'David Pawson. Perhaps you've heard of him.'

I can remember very little about that evening, just a lot of faces, and one man, it seemed, sleeping. I could not blame him. I could not have been very interesting. All I wanted to do was talk privately to David Pawson. Harry had briefly introduced me to him just before the evening got going, and he sat unobtrusively, a small, neat man, in the body of the audience while I spoke.

Then, afterwards, when they were serving cups of coffee, he came up and spoke to me quietly, explaining that he had been over-working, and he would like to talk to me at depth in the freshness of a new day, if that were possible. The next day was Saturday: it was my day off.

'Tomorrow morning?' I offered hastily.

'Good idea. Come about half-past ten, and Enid will make us some coffee. We can have the whole day to ourselves, if necessary.'

Then he said something else, and I will never forget it.

'I don't want you to take this the wrong way, but all the time you were speaking tonight, I knew that God's real purpose in bringing you down here this evening wasn't to talk to us about your job, but because God wants you and me to get together. He has business for us to do together.'

I am a good sleeper normally, but I think I had a restless night after that.

I should say that by now my overwhelming need was becoming clarified in my mind. I was seeking the experience of the baptism in the Spirit.

My reading had sharpened my understanding of what

it was God offered, and the few sincere Christian friends who tried to tell me there was no such thing as the baptism in (or of) the Spirit could not dissuade me. The evidence of the Bible seemed overwhelming.

The sending of the Holy Spirit had been prophesied through Ezekiel back in Old Testament days. In Chapter 36, verse 26, God said: 'I will give you a new heart and a new mind. I will take away your stubborn heart of stone and give you an obedient heart. I will put my spirit in you, and I will see to it that you follow my laws and keep all the commands I have given you.'

I had pondered long over that. '*I will give you* a new heart and a new mind', not '*You must develop* a new heart and a new mind.' Anybody who has ever tried to keep a New Year's resolution knows it is difficult enough to be nice to the boss even for a week. On your own, just about all you can do by trying desperately to be good and 'holy' and 'religious' is steer yourself towards a nervous breakdown, or a bout of irreversible cynicism.

Then, in the New Testament, I had found John the Baptist's promise: 'I baptise you with water to show that you have repented, but the one who will come after me will baptise you with the Holy Spirit and fire.' (Matthew 3:11). That hardly seemed like something that would slowly develop through years of endeavour.

Jesus, as well, made several promises. Just read through John.

Chapter 7: verses 38–39: 'As the scripture says, "Whoever believes in me, streams of life-giving water will pour out from his heart." Jesus said this about the Spirit, which those who believed in Him were going to receive. At that time the Spirit had not yet been given, because Jesus had not been raised to glory.'

Chapter 14: verses 15–17: 'If you love me you will obey my commandments. I will ask the Father, and he will give you another Helper, who will stay with you for ever. He is the Spirit, who reveals the truth about God.'

And John 16: verse 7: 'But I am telling you the truth: it is better for you that I go away, because if I do not go, the Helper will not come to you. But if I do go away, then I will send Him to you.'

These are just samples. Look for yourself.

These were promises Jesus made before his death, and it was not difficult to understand. While He was alive on earth, He was confined by his very humanness, his physical form. In Spirit, He could communicate to the whole universe.

During the forty days when Jesus reappeared to his followers after his death on the cross, He repeated those promises: 'But when the Holy Spirit comes upon you, you will be filled with power, and you will be witnesses for me in Jerusalem, in all Judea and Samaria, and to the ends of the earth.' (Acts 1:8)

So the giving of the Holy Spirit was to give certainty and power to these questioning, frightened and bewildered followers. The instructions were clear to the Christians: they were to tell the world. So how could you be a Christian and never share with your friends the story of Christ? It was rank disobedience. Yet to do so requires an injection of fuel that thousands of nominal Christians clearly do not possess. I knew that well enough, because I was one of those people.

I spent the whole of the next morning in deep conversation with David Pawson in the sitting room of their home. He listened to my questions, heard of my predicament, sympathised with my confusion. Before I left, he gave me this assurance: that God's Spirit did live in me, and that God would soon confirm this fact to me in some way that would be right for me.

Since that meeting, David and Enid Pawson have been cherished friends of mine.

I knew, as I drove away from their home that day, that I was close to an event that would be something, I supposed, like falling in love. Somehow, all the head-full of knowledge that I was accumulating was going to make the short, but essential, journey to my heart, and I was going to KNOW the truth with certainty.

8: *A whole new ball game*

For a long time I had been thinking about going to a
different church. Not because I did not like them at the
church I was attending: I hardly knew them, beyond a
polite greeting at the back of the church. It was probably
more my fault than theirs, but something kept holding
me back from getting my feet under the table at that
place.

It was not that I was weary of the 1662 form of service,
or did not like the alternative series. Selfishly, I merely
recognised that my own need was not being met, my
yearning to clear up my own problem and to hear
inspiring teaching on things of the Spirit.

All the years that I had intermittently been attending
churches in various parts of the country where my career
took me, all those years, it now occurred to me, I had
never heard one sermon on the Gifts of the Holy Spirit (1
Corinthians 12:8–11) or the Fruit of the Spirit (Galatians
5:22). Or, if I had, then I had not been listening.

Yet the Holy Spirit was the dynamic force that wonderfully transformed the early Christians from fearful men
to men of fire and vision after the extraordinary
happening of Pentecost (Acts 2:1–4). 'Three thousand
converts in one day!' I had written and underlined under
the sketch on page 151 of my Good News Bible. Boy,

those early Christians really saw results! It was not much like that in the churches I attended through the years. All very sonorous and tip-toeing, not that I had been convinced, either, by some of the hellfire and damnation I had heard preached from a few Welsh pulpits.

It had seemed to me that much the same spirit that pumped *hwyl* into one or two of those preachers, and the elders who loudly amen'd them, spurred them into lusty adventures in the cornfields in midweek. It was not always easy, either, to distinguish between the fervour in the chapel singing and the fervour in the four ale bar. Same hymns, either place. 'Bread of heaven' and all that.

It was not easy for me to begin to search in neighbouring churches. We had been brought up to be loyal: our parents had set us an example of loyalty, and you tried not to let them down.

I did not have Arthur Wallis's brave book, *The Radical Christian*, to guide me as to whether to stay put or move on. I wish it had been by my bedside then. No matter, very shortly after my session with David Pawson two incidents prompted my decision. The first was when I heard a particular sermon at one of the churches I had been rather attracted to. It was to a text from 1 Corinthians 14: the verses where Paul instructs the church in Corinth what form their services should take:

'When you meet for worship, one person has a hymn, another a teaching, another a revelation from God, another a message in strange tongues, and still another the explanation of what is said.' (verse 26).

It all sounded well constructed and erudite, and the sermon was delivered, as well, in an agreeable voice. I drove home feeling mildly edified, until it occurred to me that it was a lot of poppycock – not what was said but the reality of the circumstances in that church. If anyone had stood up and begun his own choice of hymn, the place would have been thrown into utter confusion.

If another had embarked on a message in strange tongues, he would have been rushed to one of the nearby institutions, I was certain.

The second incident occurred as I was leaving my own church after eight o'clock Communion one Sunday morning. 'Hey, I want a word with you!' challenged the young curate I had befriended there. 'When are you going to stop flitting round all the local churches and settle down again?'

'When I find one where they actually believe God's still in business today,' I answered spontaneously.

Before we could develop our conversation, someone else beckoned him aside, and while I waited for him to return his attention to me, a lady said to me, almost apologetically: 'I know where you'll find that sort of church. Just a mile and a half down the road.' And she told me where, in a schoolroom, behind some shops.

I decided I would give it a try the next Sunday morning.

I am not sure I was quite prepared for what I found. An Upper Room, indeed (the Ewell Fellowship has since moved to much cosier surroundings), but it was not the bare floor boards that set me back on my heels. People hugged and kissed each other when they arrived. The songs they sang, to guitar accompaniment, weren't your Hymns Ancient and Modern, but rather bouncy. And people began to clap hands to the rhythm. Then some of the women actually danced round the floor. People raised their arms, as well, as they sang.

Then, worse still, two of the men did a sort of jig together. It was all most unbecoming.

Different people began to pray, in turn. Then one of the men read a passage from the Bible. No-one had invited him to. That, would you believe, led to a discussion of sorts. After that they sang another catchy tune about being gathered in this place to worship Him. I liked the tune, but they had their arms in the air again, and that was very off-putting.

Now a hush fell on the place, and someone I could not quite see began to speak in a language that certainly was not English. 'Praying in tongues,' I reassured myself. Another person followed that with a brief message, almost as if he were God, speaking in the first person.

I glanced towards the door, wondering if I might leave early without causing too much of a stir. But I was rather hemmed in. Besides, I sensed we were getting towards the sermon, and that would be revealing, wouldn't it? Well, it was hardly notable for its rhetoric, but it was in every-day language, and very much to the point, I had to acknowledge. He seemed a decent sort of a bloke, too: looked rather athletic, and that appealed to me.

But before they all went home for the Sunday roast, they raised their arms over another of their songs, and really it was all a bit too much for me. A culture shock, I think they call it. I was not sorry I had gone along for the experience, but it was not really my cup of tea.

It is just as well I had a week to digest it all. I needed all of that. I had to admit they seemed a very happy little band of people, and not at all pushy towards me, which I welcomed. If they had been I would probably never have returned. There was something else I was willing to concede after a day or two to muse over it: that style of impromptu worship was a good deal more like the service Paul was writing about than the staid, dry, formalised routine I was used to.

Next Sunday morning I went back again. They shared communion this time, just passing round a small, brown loaf, and then handing a chalice from one to another. There could not have been more than thirty of them. It was very homely. Not a bit churchy. Yet reverent.

Before the end of the service, the minister invited anyone who wanted prayer for healing to come out, and a woman stepped forward. He laid hands on her and quietly asked Jesus to heal her. I looked for a miracle, but I did not see one. It was disappointing.

I was struck by the real concern the people showed for each other. There was nothing tepid about it. Their worship had ardour, I acknowledged to myself, and I wondered if their life-styles lived up to that all week.

Someone started up that song about being Gathered in His Name to Worship Him again, and I discovered I had remembered the tune. I liked it, only I wished they would not raise their arms in the air like that when they sang it. I was sorry no-one prayed in tongues this time, because I wanted to listen more carefully to what they were saying. The second service had not been much like the first one I had attended. This one had been gentler: there was an appealing sense of peace in the room.

For three or four Sundays I went along to investigate. At the door, they always smiled and looked happy to see me. It was all very relaxed. Most of all, I was touched by their joy for each other; and also for their caring, especially when the minister prayed over any of the sick for healing. I had found that his name was Trevor Martin, and I warmed to him. I began to look forward to seeing them on Sunday mornings. If only they would not wave their arms about.

That, I could clearly identify, was a hang-up to me: the arm-waving; and the dancing, as well. It did not seem proper in a church. But gradually I could see that I could not have it both ways: I could not want spontaneous worship in the language of our age and then jib at it when I got it. And if I was excited enough about Crystal Palace when they scored a goal to throw my hands in the air, wasn't I excited enough by God to throw my hands in the air for him?

I could not seek the supernatural Spirit of God, yet be turned off by the sound of a message in tongues.

Besides, as I well knew, speaking in tongues was utterly scriptural. I knew of Anglicans who had the gift of tongues, so it must be all right! I began to discover what the Bible had to say about lifting hands, and I soon found the exhortation in Psalm 134:2: 'raise your hands in prayer in the Temple and praise the Lord!' Then there was Isaiah 1:15, which begins: 'When you lift your hands in prayer. . . .'

Again, in his first letter to Timothy (Chapter 2:8), Paul makes the plea: 'In every church service I want the men to pray, men who are dedicated to God and can lift up their hands in prayer without anger or argument.'

As to clapping hands, Psalm 47 implores: 'Clap your hands for joy, all peoples!'

Then it occurred to me: what timid kind of love is it that never carries a man above the limitations of his own self-consciousness? As for dance in worship, I can do no better than recall the prayer of an old farmer in a tiny Welsh chapel after a dozen of the youngsters had just broken out in dance. The man, who, you might have thought, would have been mortified by such outrageous goings-on in the 'house of the Lord', prayed out: 'Thank you, heavenly Father, that the boys and girls can be so happy in this place that they want to dance for joy, instead of dancing in the discos!'

Why should I shy from these acts of worship when, all my life, I had never questioned the validity of people making the sign of the cross, or genuflecting? It was just that I had been brought up in that particular idiom of worship.

Increasingly, I felt myself warming to these people in Ewell: carpenters and plumbers, bankers, and toffs, as well. What I liked best about them, though, as I became more familiar with them, was their sense of liberation in their worship, and apparently in their lives, as well. Going to church with these people was – well, fun! Yes, fun. They seemed to live their faith through the week, too: it didn't end with bed on Sunday night.

I began to appreciate that, though theirs was eighties-style worship, it was much more Book of Acts-worship. And this next fact became firmly embedded in my thinking: that anyone desperately in need stumbling upon this group of people at worship (anyone with no background of a forbidding 'church' atmosphere) would be far less likely to be put off than by the whispered, holy huddles, and the thees and thous of many churches I had known.

Why do we have to address God as 'Thou' in the 1980s'? Well, why? Doesn't He understand the way we talk today?

And hasn't He inspired men to write any new hymns since Rock of Ages and The Church's One Foundation? They were mighty, all right, but are there no mighty songs for today's young Christians?

What's wrong with 'Jesus, How Lovely You Are', and 'Jesus Take me as I am'?

Another thing: do we have to restrict our range of musical instruments to an organ, beautiful though it is? What is wrong with drums and guitars? After all, they are the instruments of today's young people. And Hebrews 13:8 assures us that 'Jesus is the same yesterday, today and forever.'

What is so disrespectful about four thousand kids in denims and T-shirts swarming into the Royal Albert Hall for a Christian rock concert? After all, Garth Hewitt, down there on the stage, sings rock raucously, as percussion shakes the old place, and Garth is a Church of England parson.

It is not my favourite sound, but the youngsters love it. Surely the test is whether the truth of their lives lives up to the claims of their faith. What matters is that they find God sufficiently absorbing that they don't need to seek their thrills in drugs and sex and street gangs.

But why can't they have *their* music in our churches on Sundays? Or is it to be only *our* music?

Can't Cliff Richard speak for Christ as well as the Archbishop of Canterbury can?

If I believe you can play centre half for Watford and also be a Christian, as Ian Bolton is, why can't you sing pop on a stage like Dave Pope and be a Christian, which Dave is?

And why can't you be very funny in a pulpit on a Sunday, as Gordon Bailey is? Is laughter, released and infectious, an affront to God, or a gift from God wonderfully medicinal in these days of terror and stress?

For me, this was a time of my life of massive unlearning, of deeply-rooted prejudices being washed away. I began to relish the freedom. It all seemed so exciting, and so real. Reality had been what I was searching.

My mind was made up. I looked up Trevor Martin's telephone number in the local directory and invited myself along for a talk at his home. He was sensitively responsive. There was a great deal to tell him. There were many questions to be asked by both of us, and some to be answered. He listened sympathetically, and he was frank. I had been right about his looking athletic: he had played cricket. He had even supported Crystal Palace!

I told him of my discussion with David Pawson and what David had said to me. I said I wanted, above all, the assurance that I was baptised in the Spirit. I wanted to be given certainty, and I wanted things to change in my life, anxieties to fade, attitudes to go, hurts to be healed.

I did not want to be a doubter any longer.

A few weeks later, in that same comfortable lounge, Trevor prayed for me, asking God to answer me. Then he prayed quietly in tongues . . . and I began to pray in tongues with him. There was no weeping, no flooding of emotion: nothing, really, except a feeling of serenity, I knew my search was over, and I was at a new beginning.

I have not doubted since.

9: *What the papers say*

Looking back, I can see that, with that feeling of certainty, a delight grew in me to learn, and properly to understand, what God is really doing and saying. To read the Bible became like a drink from a mountain stream on a hot summer day rather than a dose of salts. My morning quiet time (usually in the bath!) developed into a haven where I could be becalmed and refuel for the demanding day ahead.

Situations began to happen round me when I wasn't looking, and afterwards I would understand with awe the hand that had been behind them.

Like the day that a friend invited me round for a coffee and chat one evening, and I got into a conversation with another guest in the house. I did not know her intimately, but I knew she had begun to attend one of the local churches and had made a profession of faith.

'What I can't stand,' she suddenly offered gratuitously, 'are charismatics, waving their arms about, and stuff like that!' (Where had I heard that before?)

'Well,' I answered, 'for a start I don't think worship is what people are labelling charismatic just because you wave your arms about and sing new choruses. A charismatic, surely, is someone who believes in the Gifts of the Spirit, as listed in 1 Corinthians 8 onwards – you know, gifts of wisdom, knowledge, faith, healing, miracles, the gift of being able to speak God's message, the ability to tell the difference between gifts that come from the Spirit and those that don't, the gift of tongues, the gift of interpretation.

That, surely, is what makes a charismatic, though it's another label, and I don't like labels.

The arm-waving ought to be a sign of that person's release from self-consciousness and inhibition, and his sheer love of God, but, of course, it can be just a show, just as lighting candles and burning incense can be just a show. I mean, if you wave your arms about on Sunday and go out with someone else's husband on Monday, it's all a sham. But God knows the truth. Surely He's the only one who can judge a person's sincerity.'

The woman suddenly lost interest in the conversation, and soon made some lame excuse and went out. I supposed she had decided I was another religious fanatic, and she did not want to waste her time! But my host looked at me open-eyed.

'I believe you've been sent here by God,' she said.

'What on earth do you mean?'

'You don't know what you've been saying,' she continued, her hand to her mouth almost in disbelief.

'What's going on? What are you talking about?' I asked.

'You don't know, do you? I mean, you don't know anything about it.'

'About what?'

'You didn't know she's being going round with someone else's husband, did you?'

No, I had not. I had no idea, not even a suspicion. If I had done, I would have been far too apprehensive to have spoken so off the cuff. That was the whole point. I could see it now. We both could. Even more important, the woman KNEW I didn't know about it.

Incidents like that began to occur more and more often.

Something else that happened was that I began to be given crystal-clear understandings of fundamental truths of the Christian faith, truths that had been shrouded in mist all those years before.

Like the matter of being 'born again'. The papers are full of it: it's a new cliché they have cottoned on to – 'born-again Christians' they write about. I doubt whether they know quite what they mean by the phrase. There was a caption under a happy picture of my friends Sue Barker and Cliff Richard in my old paper one morning. 'They are both born-again Christians' the reporter wrote.

Did that make Sue and Cliff some sort of freaks? Or did it suggest that they are in a religious cult?

The phrase, as it had suddenly become part of our everyday vocabulary, had wafted across from the United States, where, I had discovered for myself, people were forever being referred to as 'born-again Christians.' I could see clearly what it meant to the world out there. Somehow they (and the newspapers, who guide and reflect them) had to find a way to distinguish between the grey mass of people who sometimes go to church on Sundays but whose lives are no different from anybody else's on Monday, and those Christians who appeared to have taken such a change of direction that it was clearly evidenced in their lifestyle.

So 'the world out there', not understanding, has called the second group 'born-again Christians.' It is simple, and it saves getting into semantics. To be candid, I used to be put off by it myself.

Now, though, I began to see how vital the phrase really is, even if the great mass of people do not realise it. In John Chapter 3 the Bible recounts the story of a meeting betwen Jesus and a man named Nicodemus, and that is where the phrase comes from.

This Nicodemus was no ordinary Joe Soap. He was a Jewish leader: he belonged to the party called the Pharisees. So he was a religious man, and that is important to know. One night he sought out Jesus to talk to him about his God-given power to work miracles, a power he freely acknowledged that Jesus possessed.

The Bible says that Jesus answered (verse 3): 'I am telling you the truth: no-one can see the Kingdom of God unless he is born again.' (There it is, that phrase!)

You can imagine Nicodemus scratching his wise head. 'How can a grown man be born again?' he asked. 'He certainly can't enter his mother's womb and be born a second time!'

Jesus repeated: 'I am telling you the truth. No-one can enter the Kingdom of God unless he is born of water and the Spirit. A person is born physically of human parents, but he is born spiritually of the Spirit.'

That truth confirms what John himself had written at the start of his gospel: 'Some, however, did receive him and believed in him; so he gave them the right to become God's children. They did not become God's children by natural means, that is, by being born as the children of a human father: God himself was their father.' (verses 12 and 13)

So the conditions of entry are: that you have to *believe*, and you have to *accept*. Believe, that is, in the God of the Bible, and the Christ of the Bible: we don't have the right to make him the Jesus we would prefer. 'Oh, Jesus liked a good time, an odd boozy night with his mates,' says a lovely boozy pal of mine, knowingly. 'He wasn't averse to a cuddle or two with some buxom damsel!' Sorry; wrong! The Bible says that Jesus shared our human nature (Hebrews 2:14), and he was tempted in every way that we are, but *he did not sin* (Hebrews 4:15).

See what I mean?

And how can you possibly relate the dramatic act of

being born again of the Spirit (Jesus's insistence on entry into the Christian faith) with the commonly held opinion: 'I was born a Christian. This is a Christian country?' I have heard that from worthy people of far better education than I had. Some I can think of have graduated from the cream of our universities.

It simply is not so: not according to Christ himself. We do not 'become Christian' by turning up in a church for weddings and funerals, the midnight service on Christmas Eve and Easter Communion. We do not 'become Christian' by going to church every single Sunday. We do not 'become Christian' because our parents were Christians.

Some of our churches teach such a watered-down social ethic that you might think you 'become Christian' by the quantity of your good works. But if your concern is for social ethics (and it is admirable that it should be), you might just as well throw in your lot with the Lions, the Round Table, the WRVS or a political party, because they all abound with people generated by the excellent intention of helping others and improving the world.

But I remember being deeply struck by what Charles Colson, one of the Watergate ex-prisoners, said at Millmead, in Guildford, one Sunday evening when I was there. Chuck Colson had been one of Nixon's most influential aides (some said 'hatchet men'), and he knew from personal experience in the White House, and in international politics, precisely what 'the best of intentions' did to remedy the tragic state of the world today.

Colson told us that evening: 'In my prison cell, I could starkly see that the only thing that can change the course of the world is a change in men's hearts; and the only way you can change men's hearts is through the power of the Holy Spirit.'

That is what Jesus was talking about to Nicodemus: 'A person . . . is born spiritually of the Spirit.'

I could see now, with the brightest illumination, that, if you accept the word of the Bible to be true, you are not a Christian *unless* you are born again. In actual fact, Christians ought to live such changed lives – all of us – that atheists and agnostics, those people who never really think about it, and those from other faiths, should not have to describe us as 'born-again Christians', but merely by the word 'Christian'.

The Bible is utterly consistent on this point, I could see.

One of the key verses, I believe, is in 2 Corinthians 5:17–18: 'When anyone is joined to Christ, he is a new being; the old is gone, the new has come. All this is done by God, who through Christ changed us from enemies into his friends, and gave us the task of making others his friends also.'

Here is another cardinal assurance on the point: 'And we know that our old being has been put to death with Christ on the cross, in order that the power of the sinful self might be destroyed, so that we should no longer be the slaves of sin.'

Even in churches where they have not deserted the clear Biblical teaching on being 'born again', it seems to me they often omit to emphasise that this complete turn-around in our life is not dependent on *our* efforts (though we have to show God the will to start afresh), but that Christ is the vital regenerating force, through His Holy Spirit. Just look back to that verse from 2 Corinthians 5 again: 'All this is done by God,' wrote Paul.

Our part in the transaction is to make the decision to change course: that is what the Bible calls 'repentance' (repentance does not mean crying your eyes out, feeling sorry for a few hours, then doing the same thing all over again). God's part is to give His regenerating Spirit to anyone who asks.

Jesus made this promise:

'Ask, and you will receive: seek, and you will find; knock, and the door will be opened to you. For everyone who asks will receive, and he who seeks will find, and the door will be opened to anyone who knocks. . . .'

'Bad as you are, you know how to give good things to your children. How much more, then, will the Father in heaven give the Holy Spirit to those who ask him!' (Luke 11:9, 10 and 13).

The Holy Spirit, which is the power of God and without which you will be a constantly defeated Christian, is for everyone who simply asks.

If you decide to become a Christian, I implore you to take the trouble to find a church where they believe that the Holy Spirit is for today's generation and teach you how to receive. Otherwise you risk arid years in the desert. I know: I have been there myself. There is a great multitude there now; and all because the church has allowed the Christian faith to be so rationalised, so socialised, so diluted to suit every taste, that they omit to teach the parts of the Bible that tell of the supernatural power of God.

The Holy Spirit. You won't get far without Him.

What sort of church will it be?

They will be a caring people, concerned for the sick and the underprivileged, for the elderly, for all social classes and all colours of skin;

They will be a happy people, not frowning in condemnation and bound by legalism but freely enjoying the good things of life;

They will be a joyously singing people, not solemn and subdued;

They will be buoyant, many of them young people, and they will blend generously with the older members of their church, respecting their ways;

They will be out-going and involved in the local

community, looking for opportunities to relate to other Christian churches;

They will be a praying people, not constricted by prayer books and structures but talking to God as if He were in the place with them, listening;

They will be vividly expectant, believing that God will answer them in His time and His way;

They will be a people of great faith in God to break through the natural laws to alter circumstances that arise, giving miracles of healing and restoring shattered lives that no human endeavour could rebuild;

They will be a REAL people, with real problems to overcome, just like anybody else but with a sense of security and trust and peace even in times of agonising turmoil in their lives;

They will be people with creased and thumbnailed and underscored Bibles, because the Bible will be their daily reading, not a black, forbidding book that appears only on the lectern on Sundays;

They will be honest;

They will be radical;

You may not understand them at first, but you will like them, because they will be a people of quality.

And they will want to tell you about John 3:16:

'For God loved the world so much that he gave his only Son, so that everyone who believes in him may not die but have eternal life.'

Now – please – just think about that. Don't hurry on but look at it, and see if you can let the immensity of that claim somehow be absorbed into you.

'For God loved the world so much that he gave his only Son, so that everyone who believes in him may not die but have eternal life.'

It may help you to appreciate the awesome mercy of what God did if you think of the faces of the bereaved parents and wives who attended the Falklands memorial service at St Paul's Cathedral. Didn't your heart feel their pain for a moment or two? Mine did.

Multiply that sacrifice of theirs a thousand thousand times, and you begin to know what it meant for God not merely to allow his son to be crucified (because, as God, he could have worked a miracle to prevent it) but actually to plan for it to happen that way. And you begin to know what it meant for Jesus himself, who had done nothing but love people, and heal people and forgive people and give them hope, to be a willing accomplice to this greatest rescue act in the history of man.

Think of it: because Jesus died, we don't have to be weighed down by our own feelings of guilt over our wanton selfishness and wrong-doing, or by the tragic mess we are all making of the world he gave us to enjoy. (Only two days since 1945 without a war somewhere; concentration camps, barbarous terrorism in the name of religion, even; cynical exploitation and repression in quest of wealth and power or the requirements of the state; lovelessness everywhere.)

God's plan was that his own son's death, at a stroke, would wipe out all the horrendous evils of the past, the present and the future. If only we believe, we can enjoy that freedom.

It is so simple, so freely given, you almost can't credit it! Money can't buy it. Neither can our good deeds. We just have to get to a point of belief that God so loved the world he gave his only begotten son. . . .

If we find we really do believe – not just give a grudging acquiescence – how can we resist?

I can only speak for myself. One reason I took so long was that I didn't think I could keep it up. (I was right: I couldn't, and I still can't. Ask my closest family. Ask the people I work with. But at least I can make an honest try; and when I blow it, I know that I have a wealth of Christian friends to pick me up again with their love and understanding; and I know that the power of God, His Holy Spirit, lives in me and is there to refresh me.)

Also, I kept pointing to the example of so-called Christians, and their hypocrisy (instead of looking at myself, and looking at the example of Jesus.)

I was too proud, as well. Too concerned at what other people might say about me. ('He's got religion, you know!'). So God had to be patient till the events of my life had destroyed my pride, and I had nothing to lose.

I wonder what your particular blockage is? All I can say is: *dare* to take a step in faith, and join the team. Have you got the guts to stand up and be counted?

Have you got the time not to?

10: *In the team*

George Foreman had the guts to humble himself enough to become a Christian: he was heavyweight boxing champion of the world. Margaret Court did, too: she was the best tennis player in the world. You don't have to be the best at anything, though, to be of more use to God than you will probably ever know. Where was it I read that when a famous person kneels to pray, he is no bigger than anybody else? It is certainly true.

In some ways, it may be more difficult to yield yourself to God if you get your name in the papers, and people want your autograph. To be a success in sport, for instance, it is fundamental that you must believe in your own ability. Or so we are told.

Coaches drum it into you: 'If *you* don't think you're any good, son, no-one else will!'

In sport, too, you are encouraged to be selfish, which is the very opposite motivation of the person to whom 'Jesus is Lord.' 'Look, it's you or her. There's no sentiment in sport. You've got to go in and kill!'

No, no mercy. 'The left winger's a coward, so go in hard in the first five minutes, and put him over the touchline. You won't hear from him again, I promise you!'

Or: 'When he got cramp in the fifth set, you should

have given him the drop shot and lob, instead of rushing round the net to ask if he was all right!'

Or: 'You stand your ground, my son, till the umpire lifts his finger.'

Sport, at professional level especially, can be very tough, and often very lonely.

Alan West is a successful footballer. He embarked on his Soccer career at Turf Moor, in Burnley, nursery of some of the finest players Britain has produced. He won an FA Youth Cup winners' medal when he was with Burnley, and in 1971 he played for England's under-23 team against Wales. Later on, Burnley sold him to Luton Town for a fee of £100,000, and, after eight years at Luton, he was transferred to Millwall.

One summer, while he was on Luton's books, Alan decided to earn some extra money and see something of the world by playing for Minnesota Kicks, in the North American Soccer League. Of course, he took Cathie, his pretty wife, out there with him.

During their stay with Minnesota that year, he was given a fortnight's break during America's bi-centennial celebrations, so he and Cathie thought it would be a good idea to visit her parents, who had emigrated to New Zealand. They had not seen each other for a few years.

In fact, Cathie's mother and father had made a fresh start to their lives by crossing the world. It was an attempt to shore up their marriage. They had undergone many difficulties in their lives. In letters home to England, they had explained that they had become Christians, so Alan and Cathie boarded the plane to New Zealand not a little apprehensively. They felt it was good for Cathie's parents to have found a faith, 'but there was nothing in it for us.'

In New Zealand, for the first time, they met 'real' Christians, and, frankly, they were impressed. Alan remembers that he and Cathie had the intuitive feeling that these people had more meaning in their lives; more love and joy, as well. They began to ask questions, and Alan picked up a Bible to check out a few things that were being said.

One evening, after two hours of serious questioning in a friend's house, Cathie told Alan she believed in the truth of what these Christians were saying. Alan recalled to *Family* magazine's David Hall some years later: 'She was emotional and upset, and I was stubborn and proud.'

'Yet' wrote David Hall (himself a sports writer and a Christian, though not in that order) 'when Cathie made a decision to be a Christian and asked Jesus Christ into her life, Alan was alongside her doing the same.'

Now, just imagine what was going through Alan West's mind in the weeks ahead. What on earth were the Luton footballers going to say when he told them? They would probably decide he had gone off his head. And how would he break the news to them, anyway? Before, he had been no different from any other young man, not particularly selective in his language, for a start. Now, gradually, it was all changing.

Their instinctive reaction to the Good News that had been implanted in the hearts of this very normal couple was to shout it from the hilltops, share it with everybody. It was too good to keep to themselves. Besides, Jesus had specifically instructed his followers to spread the news to the whole world. If He was to be their Lord, they had to be obedient.

What Alan and Cathie West found was that, stage by stage, they realised how God could use their particular personalities to tell others about their new beginning. They resumed their lives in Luton with a growing faith inspiring them, and altering their focus on things, as well.

Their friends began to notice it, and one of the players

came to the point one day at the Luton Town ground. 'Hey, Westie!' he challenged. 'You've changed so much! What's happened?' Alan took a deep breath and explained. Before long, one of the local newspapers heard about it and made headlines of what had happened in the life of the Luton Town captain. So now it was everyone's news.

Naturally, he took some ribbing. 'Come on, West, get your Bible out!' a stentorian voice would bellow from the terraces. Or (if he was not having a particularly good game): 'Haven't you been praying, then?' Alan learned to take it. There was another side to the coin, anyway: many Luton supporters sent him notes saying they were Christians, too, and they were praying for him. That was real encouragement.

Alan and Cathie tried a few churches in the town and eventually joined the Elim Pentecostal Church in Luton, where he is now a deacon, and that brought them not only into a position to receive teaching but into a new circle of friends. These were friendships of a different texture than they had known before.

Nowhere in the Bible does it say it will be easy when you become a Christian. On the contrary, the warning is to take up our cross every day. For Alan West, his daily cross included the kind of pressures that people outside the sporting world may not appreciate. One of these difficulties, he admits, is how to react to defeat. A football club's dressing room is a grim place when the wound of defeat is still open, and there can be outbursts of recrimination.

Alan does not like losing, but since he became a Christian he does not get depressed the way some players do, or react the way some do. It is easy to mistake his calm for indifference.

By the time Alan was transferred to Millwall, it was fairly common knowledge in the game that he was a

Christian. ('Westie, you fouled a bloke today. It's three Hail Marys for you!) So he felt his priority, as a new arrival at The Den, was to establish his credibility as a professional with his new team mates: 'I needed to gain their respect.'

Soon there was a 'Christians in Sport' dinner near Watford, with Cliff Richard singing and sharing his beliefs, and Alan was able to invite the whole club along, with their wives and girl friends. A party of about 26 made the trip, to join up with footballers from Tottenham, Watford, Luton, Newport and other clubs. They listened intently to what former professsional footballers like Ritchie Powling and Derek Jefferson had to say about the difference in their lives since they became Christians.

(Just a year earlier, a young goalscorer, Wayne Entwistle, had been taken along to a similar 'Christians in Sport' dinner in Warrington, and Wayne had subsequently made up his mind that this was the real truth about life, and he, too, became a Christian.)

And so Alan West's ministry among professional footballers continues. He often waits till the other players open up conversations with him, and then he answers their questions. Once, on a two-hour coach journey back south from Sheffield, about half a dozen of his team mates got into a discussion about the Christian faith. 'We got through the lot,' said Alan – 'the second coming, the virgin birth, the lot!'

Ordinary young men discussing fundamental truth together, prepared to lay aside prejudices and have their ideas cleared of misconceptions. Nothing 'religious', in the forbidding, intimidation sense that the word 'religious' has become known, but openly and seriously.

I said at the start of this chapter, that George Foreman, the former heavyweight champion of the world, is a Christian. I heard about Foreman from Colin Hart, who writes so perceptively on sport in *The Sun*. Colin always found Foreman disagreeable: worse than that, he wrote about him as 'mean-minded, rude, arrogant and downright belligerent.' That, at least, was the impression Colin had of him right up to the last time they had come across each other, in Africa.

Seven years later, Colin Hart and the rest of the boxing-writer corps were in Houston, Texas, to cover a fight, and heard about the 'new' George Foreman, now preaching at a small chapel close to the airport. Colin was so intrigued that he arranged to meet Foreman especially. He wrote afterwards:

'When he walked through the door of the restaurant, he wrapped his giant hand round mine in the warmest of greetings. I couldn't believe that this once surly and exceedingly menacing monster was George Foreman . . .

'The transformation is incredible. Now he is a serene and happy individual who has found peace of mind thanks to a spiritual awakening.'

Foreman told Colin Hart that, at first, he thought he could be a fighting evangelist giving glory to God in the ring, but the more he thought about it, he simply could not fight any more. At 32 years of age, he still received tempting offers to return to the ring, the kind of temptations that, sadly, Muhammed Ali was unable to resist, but when he even tried to make a fist his fingers 'just turn into a wave.'

George Foreman, 6-ft 4-ins tall and weighing 18-stone, used to think only cissies read the Bible. Today he lives by its truth.

You would hardly call Stan Smith a cissie, though he is not quite the mountainous shape of Foreman. Neither is Stan a spineless 'wet' in need of a psychological prop to keep him standing up. He is, of course, the former Wimbledon and United States tennis champion, a man whose quiet integrity and calm have been a beacon to many people through the turbulent years in which tennis so excitingly grew into a major global sporting industry once it had rid itself of what the late Herman David denounced as 'the living lie' of bogus amateurism.

For eleven years, a span that only the legendary Bill Tilden has equalled, Stan Smith manfully represented the United States in the Davis Cup, an experience that many players testify is even more draining on the nerves than playing in great championship finals.

Stan is respected by the other pros. on the tournament circuit for many qualities, which is one of the reasons they elected him one of the leaders of their own association, the ATP. One of those qualities is that he never makes excuses. I remember Ray Moore, one of the players, saying to me one day: 'You see Stan lose a match, then head straight for the locker room, and sit there all alone with an ice pack on his elbow. He never complains about it, but all the guys know the pain he gets all the time.'

Another of Stan Smith's virtues is his unflappability, and it was this, tested beyond most men's endurance, that once led to a life-changing experience for another champion, Dennis Ralston. It happened in 1972. Dennis Ralston was captain of the United States team due to play Romania in (of all places) Bucharest in what used to be called the challenge round of the Davis Cup. To have to play Ilie Nastase and Ion Tiriac, at their peak, on a slow clay court in their own country was just about the most daunting prospect any team could face, but the American team of Smith, Tom Gorman and Eric van Dillen flew into the Romanian capital ready to do just that.

Impartial witnesses to what happened in that match even today find themselves enraged by the memory of the behaviour on and round the court. They recall that the neutral referee, Enrique Morea, admitted that he was afraid for his life, the crowd were so violently partisan. Some people who were there believe that had Morea taken the kind of disciplinary action he should have done, there could have been serious disorder.

In that incendiary atmosphere, the final began with Nastase playing Smith. It was Nastase's city, Nastase's kind of court, certainly not Smith's. But Smith won that match 11–9, 6–2, 6–3. One-nil to the United States.

In the second singles, Tiriac then beat Gorman in five sets. That made it 1-all. Next, in the doubles, Smith and van Dillen beat Nastase and Tiriac in three sets. 2–1 to the United States. But Dennis Ralston knew that Smith would have to beat Tiriac in the next match if America were to win, because the fifth rubber was between Nastase and Gorman, and Gorman had never beaten Nastase in 17 previous meetings.

It was all up to Stan Smith, and, from his captain's chair at the side of the court, while the crowd howled and abused, and some of the line calling almost drove the American players to distraction, Dennis Ralston could only sit there, powerless, gripped with tension, and watch.

Well, the records show that Smith beat Tiriac 6–0 in the fifth set. Ralston remembers that it was 'absolutely unbelievable.'

Now this happened at a period in Dennis's life when he was vaguely conscious that all was not well within him. He had been a professional tennis player a long time – Wimbledon singles finalist against Manuel Santana back in 1966 – and all the travelling had taken its toll on him. What had helped, no doubt, to bring him to this point of awakening was the fact that his wife, Linda, had already become a Christian, and he had been sensitive to the change in her life.

Sitting there near the umpire's chair through the torrid battles of Bucharest, Dennis Ralston recognised 'that

Stan Smith had something I certainly didn't.' So he made a point of talking to him after the tie was finished, talking of deep things, and he began to have some inkling of the source of Stan's security.

'After we got back to the States,' Dennis recalls, 'I went four nights running to hear an evangelist at Linda's church, Porter Barrington. He talked about steps to salvation, but I felt that somehow I couldn't be forgiven. That would be too much to handle – that the slate could be wiped clean.'

So in the secret caverns where a man wrestles with his troubled thoughts, Dennis Ralston searched to grasp the full implication of the stupendous claim that Christians make for Jesus Christ: that, somehow, on the bleak cross at Calvary, cruelly beaten till his flesh was ripped open, rejected and ridiculed, with nails hammered through his hands and feet, He settled for all time the massive debts of generations past, present and future.

So simply that it was a truth too massive properly to comprehend, man had merely to accept, by an act of faith, that he was made 'not guilty' and live in obedience in that light. Dennis had only to say 'Yes'; and he did. Today, he is one of the most mature Christians in the tennis world.

11: *Running to God*

The boy Tom Farrell was sure of two things: he could run, and he wanted to play football for Everton. He knew he could run when he was sent to live in the country, near Ellesmere, during the war, and he went raiding apple orchards with the rest of the gang. The others, the local farm boys, used to get caught, but Tom was so quicksilver he was over the hedges and away while enraged and panting pursuers gave up the chase, cursing and threatening into the clean country air.

He knew he wanted to play outside right for Everton when he used to stand with the other lads in the boys' pen at Goodison Park on Saturday afternoons, marvelling at the skills of Eddie Wainwright, Wally Fielding and Harry Catterick. The dreams he dreamed there!

Tom Farrell could play, all right. He soon demonstrated that at Liverpool Collegiate High School, where he attended, and where the captain of football was a boy called Rossiter, fast and rangy and deadly in front of goal. Rossiter scored eleven goals in one game for Tom's school, and everyone knew he would be a famous Soccer star one day.

He wasn't. Leonard Rossiter, instead, became a brilliantly gifted actor, whose sense of comedy and timing

93

made him one of the most instantly recognised television faces. Tom and Len have kept in touch all this time.

Tom's sights were blinkered to all but his ambition to play for Everton, and one of the best times of the week was Sunday afternoon, because Sunday afternoons were 'footy times'. You spent every Sunday afternoon playing football at Sefton Park. It would never have occurred to Tom that Sunday might be a day for churchgoing: his family were no different from thousands of English middle-class families. Tom used to have to go to Sunday school as a small boy, but his parents were not church-goers themselves. You just did not talk about God in the Farrell household.

Tom thought religion was for old people, if he thought about it at all. So, being this sort of boy he was surprised when, one day, the year he started at Collegiate, a friend invited him to come along to a Bible class one Sunday afternoon. He decided to go, as much out of curiosity as anything, but he had hardly got his foot inside the door when he was deeply impressed by the way in which some – not all – of the people there talked about Jesus Christ. Jesus obviously meant a great deal to them. The Bible class turned out to be part of the Crusaders, he discovered, and Tom found himself being drawn by what he heard at their meetings.

If they had not been such good times for him, he would have been back to Sefton Park like a shot.

An Irishman was the local Crusader-leader. His name was James Belford, and his quiet, unobtrusive friendliness was something that Tom Farrell grew to value. Mr Belford always made sure Tom would be there when the Crusaders met.

About a year after that first Bible class Tom attended, the Crusaders had a summer camp in Beaumaris, on Anglesey, and Tom went along. Every evening, in a marquee, a man called Alan Pratt, who played Rugby for Leicester Tigers and for Leicestershire, would talk to the boys, and Tom found himself getting there earlier and earlier so that he could find a place nearer and nearer the front. One night, towards the end of the camp, he talked to them on Matthew 11:28.

Tom Farrell always remembers that verse in the language he heard it then: 'Come unto me all ye that labour and are heavy laden, and I will give you rest.' It seemed to speak directly to him that the night. 'With all the progress I had made at Soccer, I knew I was very self-oriented, extremely ambitious for myself. I just wanted to play for Everton. But I knew that the Tom Farrell I had to live with wasn't a very nice person to have around. I was so restless, and I think I realised by now that life wasn't going to make sense unless someone could take hold of me, and take away the rubbish.'

Later that night, in the pitch black of the tent he shared with some other boys, and without them being aware as they lay curled up asleep, Tom hunted for his Bible, found that text again, and silently asked Jesus to be his saviour 'Next morning,' he recalls, 'I simply knew something was different. I knew something very definite had happened. No haloes or wings had appeared, but something inside me said that everything was all right.'

They told him he must not keep this important news a secret: that he must share it with his friends, so when he got home to Liverpool, to his grandmother's house where he was staying, he immediately picked up the telephone and shouted excitedly: 'Mr Belford, I've become a Christian!' He had an ulterior motive for shouting it: it meant his grandmother heard the news, and he had been nervous about breaking it to her!

Sport remained important to Tom. By his mid-teens he was not only playing Soccer but Rugby, as well, and he had also won a place in the school athletics team. Soon, athletics was his clear priority. After Derek

Johnson had devastatingly beaten him in the All-England school 440-yards championships, the man who became Tom's coach, Denis Watts, persuaded him to concentrate his talents on the 440-yards hurdles, instead. Tom had to develop patience and resourcefulness as he persevered with hurdling at the various Royal Air Force camps he was stationed at during his National Service. As a Christian and an athlete, he was greatly influenced by Eric Liddell, about whom the film 'Chariots of Fire' was recently made with such success.

Like Liddell, Tom made the decision that he would not compete on Sundays, and thereby hangs a tale.

He was chosen to run in the NATO Air Forces athletics championships in Brussels, but it was a one-day meeting, and that day was to be a Sunday, so he said he could not take part. Later, for some reason, they altered the date to a Saturday, and Tom was elated. It would be the first international he had ever competed in.

He remembers that extraordinary day like this –

'I scraped through my heat. There was no other word for it. When it came to the final, I was drawn on the outside lane, of all places, and when we lined up I had a big black American on one side of me, and the Belgian champion was there, as well. Honestly, I was scared to death. I thought I would be beaten out of sight, humiliated, almost.

'I didn't even hear the shout "Prêts", but something told me to get up into the set position. As I came round the bend, much to my surprise, I couldn't see anybody at all! Then, as I came into the last hurdle, the Belgian champion drew alongside, and all I could see was the camera flashes, as the Press photographers popped away at their pictures. Nothing else but flashes of light. I hit the last hurdle hard, and I won by the skin of my vest, no more!'

He ran 15 yards faster than he had ever run in his life

that day. He still believes that, as with Eric Liddell, God honoured the stand he had made. Yet Tom Farrell had never intended his refusal to run on a Sunday should become a matter of undue importance. He had not wanted to be known as the athlete who wouldn't run on Sundays, and in recent years, anyway, he has run in the London Marathon on a Sunday.

When he left the RAF and went to Loughborough to do PE, with the idea of becoming a games teacher, he nevertheless, as a matter of courtesy, let the international team manager, Jack Crump, know that he did not want to compete on Sundays, and he remembers that he had nothing but helpful respect from Mr Crump and the other athletes of his time, men like Derek Ibbotson, Gordon Pirie, Derek Johnson, Arthur Rowe and Peter Radford. His decision certainly cost him a place in two internationals in 1955, but he ran in the 400-metre hurdles in the 1956 Melbourne Olympics, and the 800-metres in the Rome Olympics four years later.

He won the AAA's 400-metres hurdles title in 1957 and broke the British record the same year, against the Soviet Union.

He became a schoolmaster because he felt that God could use a person as much in that calling as in any other. It was some years later, when he had married Liz, and they had a family of three – Sarah, James and Mark – that, though in worldly terms there was every possible reason for Tom Farrell not to, with Liz's support, he studied for ordination.

He made a real impact on the boys as chaplain to Dulwich College, and today Tom Farrell, a smiling, warm man who almost ran *into* God, is vicar of Wonersh, near Guildford, in Surrey.

To him, the text that had opened a shutter of light in his life had been from Matthew's Gospel. For the American tennis player, Betsy Nagelsen, it was a verse from Paul's epistle to the Romans. For each person, God has a different touch, and a different time, and it is up to them whether they respond, as Tom Farrell did, and as Betsy did.

She was 16, and she was doing her Christmas shopping in St Petersberg, Florida. She needed to buy just one more present. It was for her mother. In a bookstore, she thumbed through a Bible. She opened it up at Romans 8 and verse 28, and she read to herself: 'For we know that in all things God works for good with those who love him.'

'Hmm', thought Betsy to herself.

A couple of weeks later a friend invited her mother to a Bible study, and Betsy decided to go with her for company. The speaker talked about Romans 8:28. Another spark had been lit, and Betsy Nagelsen's walk had begun. It has often been difficult for her, particularly, she admits, trying to equate her faith as a Christian girl to winning tennis matches. 'Either I get overly concerned with trying to win because I feel God's given me a talent that I must use to my utmost, or else I leave it *all* to Him, thinking it doesn't matter how I do.'

Betsy will admit that she has also had difficulties in aligning her attitude to rivals to the attitude of love a Christian should have to everybody. After a long time of wrestling with this, she came to the conclusion that the truth was she was *too* competitive, and that merely had the effect of making her even more tense on court. She faced up to the truth that she found it difficult really to like the girls who were her keenest rivals for places in American teams, or for positions on the computer ranking list. She identified to herself that she was covering up by pretending she was casual, but it was a charade.

Betsy Nagelsen is one of the most transparently good people I have ever met in sport, and yet she knows from personal experience that, unless we daily stand before God and honestly look for His approval or admonition, we can subtly drift off course. Obedience is a warfare some of us avoid by any subterfuge. It is easy to convince ourselves that we are being obedient if we are merely obeying in the areas that are simple for us, but God wants His way with every bit of us, and that sometimes hurts.

One of the greatest needs of the travelling sportsmen is to have a sound base in a live church fellowship, where they can be nobody, where they be candid about their fears and their failures, and where they can lovingly be honed. With the best possible motives, they can seek to live their Christian lives off a diet of cassettes and paperbacks, but they can never adequately compensate for the regular teaching and discipling they would get as ever-present members of a church where there is real life and growth.

There should be concern, as well, for the demands that are constantly made on the Christian sports stars. It is understandable that churches should want to use familiar and popular personalities to spread the Good News to a world-out-there that is intimidated by church buildings and 'religious' language, but what is just one well-intended invitation from one group can be one of dozens that clutter up the hotel room of the visiting sports star and which threaten to overwhelm him.

There is a time, after all, for all seasons.

Including a time to 'be still and know that I am God.' (Psalm 46:10).

And including a time for deep searching, which can only be done with the calm, caring help of a few friends who share your deepest anxieties and aspirations.

As Psalm 139 (verses 23 and 24) put it:
'Examine me, O God, and know my mind;
test me, and discover my thoughts.

Find out if there is any evil in me
and guide me in the everlasting way.'

In still and honest examination we will best be able to identify all the thoughts that swirl in subterranean caverns, untreated hurts and frustrations that alarmingly break the surface of our carefully cultivated public face only when the pressure is on.

By faith and obedience, though, we may receive what Paul calls the fruit of the Spirit in Galatians 5:22–23 – 'love, joy, peace, patience, kindness, goodness, faithfulness, humility and self-control.' How is that for an alternative to a life of endless turbulence, and such a fear of quiet times alone that anything at all – the radio, the TV – simply has to be switched on, because the stillness is a haunting thing.

It takes time, and the travelling sportsman may need more of it, but, as Paul puts it in Philippians 3, verse 12: 'I do not claim that I have already succeeded or have already become perfect. I keep striving to win the prize for which Jesus Christ has already won me to himself.'

12: *Something more*

Tennis has grown from a game played on vicarage lawns by genteel people into a vast commercial enterprise that can provide, for the boy or girl from small-town beginnings, a pathway to fame and riches. There are things rather more enticing than cucumber sandwiches at the end of a day's tennis in the eighties. The combined prize money available on the official men's and women's tournament circuits in 1983 was roughly fourteen million pounds.

In 1982, by the time she was 17 years of age, the American girl Andrea Jaeger had already earned half a million pounds in prize money alone. This does not include income from fashion houses who make her dresses, sporting goods manufacturers who pay her to use their particular brand of racket, and umpteen other endorsements waiting to be negotiated by smart business agents. The most successful woman player in the game in 1982, Martina Navratilova, made about threequarters of a million pounds from tournament winnings alone. In her young life, Martina's prize money haul is already not far short of two million pounds. That is more than any professional sportswoman has made in any kind of game.

The pickings are phenomenal. Tennis stars are flattered, cosseted, revered. They fly across the world the way most ordinary people might take the train to the nearest town. They stay in the most luxurious hotels. Everywhere they go, they are recognised like film stars. Schoolgirls dream of the world of fantasy that can be theirs if only they learn to play tennis the way the champions do on the centre court at Wimbledon.

One such girl was Sue Barker, at home in Paignton, in Devon.

The first time I ever saw her was at the Palace Hotel in nearby Torquay. It was a winter Saturday, and that afternoon two of the best-known tennis players in the world were due to play in the final of an indoor tournament, the Dewar Cup, on the covered courts alongside the hotel.

With Fred Perry, I was to do the commentary for World of Sport, on London Weekend Television, and I spent a couple of hours in the morning doing my research on the two players. You always need to check on things likes umpires' names, and where the ball girls come from, as well. You can then scatter these gems of information before the viewers as if you knew everything there was to know about everyone who moved near the court.

In the little professional's office beneath the courts sat the pipe-smoking figure of one of my favourite people in tennis, Arthur Roberts. He always seemed to me as much a philosopher as a tennis coach, yet coach he most certainly was, based at the hotel, and responsible for producing a whole string of international players, like Angela Mortimer, Mike Sangster, Joan Curry, and his own son Paddy. If Arthur Roberts said someone had ability at the game, then you took notice, because his record proved that he had an uncanny knack of spotting talent.

'Got anyone good up your sleeve these days, Arthur?' I asked him that morning.

'Yes, mate,' he answered chummily, sucking at his pipe. 'I think I have. Keep your eyes open this afternoon. There'll be a little blonde kid ball-girling at the net. You won't be able to miss her. She'll be so alert and keen, she'll stand out a mile. Her name's Sue Barker, and she's going to go a long way.'

I mentioned her to our producer, and during our transmission of the final that afternoon, as the two stars were towelling down at the net, he told one of his cameramen to get a close-up of the blonde ball-girl kneeling at the net. 'There she is, Gerry,' he told me over my earphones.

To the viewers I said: 'That girl's going to be a famous player herself one day, they say. Her name's Sue Barker, and she's one of the best young players in Britain.'

She became one of the three best players in the world, in fact. That was her official ranking for a short time in 1977. By the time she was 22 years of age, she had been in the semi-finals at Wimbledon, and she had won the French Open. She was a regular member of Britain's Wightman Cup and Federation Cup teams. Her blonde hair, her outdoor good looks, the freshness of her personality, her burning tenacity on the tennis court had made her a person instantly recognised in the streets, courted by newspapers, radio and television. She was earning over £100,000 a year even then. Her income was such that she became, for 4½ years, a tax exile in the United States of America, which meant that she was able to keep most of what she earned.

She had a car, a home in the States, investments, a business manager to handle her money. She stayed at the Plaza in Manhattan. She flew in Concorde. Sue Barker had everything. Since those beginnings in Torquay, she had blinkered her vision to anything else but winning more amd more tennis matches. And she won them. Her forehand blazed her a trail round the world.

If you have everything that money and success can give you, then you have happiness, logic argues; but happiness can be a surface thing. In your quiet times with yourself, you need a deeper sense of well-being and security: what some people define as 'peace'. When Sue was alone in hotel rooms, shut off from the clamour of the back-slappers, the applause of the crowd, the excited press of the newsmen in their interview rooms, the flattering eye of the television camera, she was nagged by a feeling that there was something more.

She found herself pondering on little things, like the time at Wimbledon in 1976, when Alan Godson had materialised before her from the haze of faces, beamed that challenging smile of his, and asked with a point of his finger: 'Why do you wear that cross round your neck? What does it mean to you?'

Sue felt embarrassed, which is not an unusual reaction to the Godson approach, and quickly retorted: 'I went to a convent.' That night, when she went to bed, she took off that necklace, and she did not wear it again for four years.

In fact, she had attended the Marist Convent, in Paignton, from the age of five until she became a full-time tennis player. There, she recalls, religious instruction was 'just another lesson'. It might have been history or geography. Similarly, occasionally going to Christ Church, in Paignton, on Sundays was 'the right thing to do.'

What she outstandingly remembered from the teaching she received at school was that if she had done anything wrong, she could be forgiven. 'It was sort of taking – not giving. It didn't have any real impact on my life at all.'

Sue certainly was touched, though, by Sister Pascal.

'She never actually taught me, because she was elderly. She had a reputation for being a bit of a dragon, but she showed me a lot of love, and I'd never really experienced that from outside the family or circle of close friends. When I was away she would write me lovely little letters, with passages from the Bible. It must have had some effect, because I used to seek her out. She was someone I could talk to who didn't seek my company simply because I was a young tennis player.

'Before she died, when I was 17 or 18, she gave me a medallion and told me to keep it close to me. She said, "Jesus is close to you." I thought I had lost her when she died, but it's wonderful now that I know I haven't lost her, and that she's still praying for me.'

Things began to come to a head in Sue's life at the end of 1977. She was depressed about not being able to fly home from America because she had already used up her allocation of 63 days in Britain. The endless stress of travel and competition had drained her, and in Japan she was discovered to have anaemia. She was advised not to play for three months.

She arranged with her parents that they would meet up for a holiday in southern Spain, near Marbella. It was there that Sue began some deep thinking about her life. Alan Godson's remark to her that day at Wimbledon had made her feel, she says, 'inadequate'. She began to look at people round her to see if they, unlike her, were fulfilled. She kept thinking: 'I was in the semi-finals at Wimbledon this year, and yet . . . is this all there is?'

Answers did not come at once. She admits now that they might have come sooner if she had been less reluctant to talk to girls like Betsy Nagelsen when they were playing together in the same tournaments. Stubbornly, Sue did not want to admit to herself, or to anyone else, that other people had something she lacked. Besides, at the time she was unclear exactly what a Christian was.

'I suppose, if anyone had asked, I'd have said I was a Christian.'

Her brief conversation with Alan Godson had spurred her to begin to pray. She had every reason: the most important thing in her life, her tennis, had been going wrong. She found certain relief in 'just speaking out how I felt.'

'Then, suddenly, I thought to myself: "If I don't believe Jesus is alive, and able to work in my life, why do I pray?" ' She felt a lot closer to the truth by now, and in April, 1978, she was christened at Christ Church, in Paignton. It turned out to be just a beginning. In the summer, two years later, on holiday at the Spanish seaside resort of Sitges, near Barcelona, leaving some friends' house, she bent to pat their dog, and it bit her twice, under her right eye and down the side of her face. She had to have fifteen stitches round the eye, and for seven hours she could not see out of that eye. It turned out to be shock.

'Mum came into my bedroom that night and said: "Listen, something good will happen from this. God's in charge of this. He makes things happen for the best." '

In her fright (because, after all, it could have meant the end of her career) Sue sensed a feeling of anger with God for allowing such an accident to happen at the one time she was searching for Him. In her bedroom that same night she realised that her mother was praying. She had never heard her pray like that before, and it moved her.

'So I sort of said: "OK, Lord, if you're in control, please give me my sight back, and I'll make more of an effort to look for you." I suppose it was a deal, really. Well, seven hours later, I did get my sight back, and, for the first time in my life, I really said Thank You to God. It was a very humbling experience.'

'He didn't leave me alone after that, and when I went

106

back to the tournament circuit, in America, one day in a hotel in Seattle I met two pop groups, and I got into conversation with a Christian from each of them. One of them was Cliff Richard's band (though Cliff was not there); another was Eric Clapton's group. That turned out to be really significant for me, because I'd felt somehow too worldly to be a Christian – the way I liked to dress, for instance – but when I met this chap he didn't look like anyone I'd met in a church. When I listened to their experience of Christian life, I knew then that I wasn't really a Christian. When they talked about Jesus, you could see the love in them. It really shook me. I learned a lot that week, as well.'

Another influence at that time was the physiotherapist to the British tennis teams, John Matthews. John was giving Sue treatment for a thigh strain, and he used to talk to her quietly about what it meant to him to be a Christian. Sue could sense that it was as if God wanted to keep her near His family: Betsy Nagelsen one week in Deer Creek, playing doubles with her; John Matthews as Sue prepared for the Daihatsu indoor tournament at the Brighton Centre. It was there, in Brighton that week, where she beat Tracey Austin, then Barbara Potter and finally Mima Jausovec to win the tournament with millions watching on television, that Sue was sure that things were happening inside her.

The day after her triumph in the final, Alan Godson phoned her to say 'Well done'. Their conversation seemed to last for ever. By the end of that week Sue had become a Christian. Now she had no doubt about it. All on her own, in her own home, she was overwhelmingly aware of the love of God, and she could only respond.

Since that day, Sue has known many of the good and the difficult things that confront a baby Christian. She has experienced great joy deep inside her. She has sought to learn from the Bible with the same intensity that made her a great tennis player: she has wanted, hungrily, all that God has to give, so that she can have His power working in her life: she has found friendship of a depth she seldom experienced before.

She has occasionally been disconcerted by the amount of attention she has had from within the Christian family: so many invitations to speak that, added to the demands of a tennis player's tournament schedule and practice requirements, at times threatened to confound her. She has been hurt by the negative response of some people to her statement of faith. Particularly this has been so when they have pointed to her consequent slump on the tennis ranking list and blamed it on her decision to become a Christian.

It has been a time of discovery, and not all of that discovery has been easy to take. She had to find a new motivation for winning, because all her life she had been powered by intense feelings of rivalry across the net. Now she could not call on those feelings any more. By the time she reached Wimbledon 1982, happy in Cliff's company and feeling that 'it was all in God's hands, so I didn't *have* to win any more', her performances on court were causing general concern.

On the evening of the middle Sunday of that Wimbledon, Sue and Cliff Richard, and several Christian tennis players, including the Mayer brothers, Steve Denton and Betsy Nagelsen, attended a 'Christians in Sport' service at the Millmead Centre in Guildford, and during the service I interviewed Sue about the recent course of her life. The packed congregation immediately warmed to her honesty.

In the melee of people round her at the service's end were two boys. One of them asked Sue: 'Why do Christians have to be second best?' Their innocent enquiry lingered long with her, and as 1982 neared its end, Sue

Barker resolved that she would find an alternative way to win at tennis.

Time will tell whether she succeeds. As with all people in the public eye, she is a target of many influences, many who would seek to manipulate. Life in the goldfish bowl of international fame may look appealing from the outside, but from within it is often a good deal less than that.

Sensibly, she is taking her life day by day. 'I don't really know what God wants of me. He hasn't made it clear yet,' she says. But she knows she now has something more.

Jackie Dyson has something more, as well. Yet, back in 1958, at the Commonwealth Games in Cardiff, Jackie Dyson, then just 15, stood on the podium at the swimming pool, leaned forward and had a silver medal hung round her neck after the final of the women's 220-yards breast-stroke, and thought there was nothing more the world could possibly give her.

Standing there with her on the rostrum were two other English girls, Anita Lonsborough, wearing the gold medal, and Christine Gosden, with the bronze, and the band played Land of Hope and Glory – 'and we were all crying, Anita and I with excitement, Christine, I think, with disappointment.'

For Jackie, it was the reward for hours of self-discipline and training: training at Kingston Baths, in Surrey, between 7.30 and 8.30 before school five mornings a week, training during the lunch hour, then more training in the evenings, or else competition at galas up and down the country. The public never sees the sheer slog of it.

Jackie's boy friend, even in her teenage, was Derek Brant, himself a club swimmer in Kingston, keen on just about every sport. They used to go to church together, even, and helped teach at Sunday-school, 'though we really had no idea at all!', she now acknowledges. She was a bright, effervescent girl even then, who knew where she was going, and at 17 years of age she had the savvy to recognise that she had reached her peak, so she gave up.

At 21 she married Derek Brant. Once again, Jackie thought she had everything: 'a good marriage, lovely parents, a nice house in a quiet cul-de-sac in Thames Ditton, two cars (including Derek's E-type Jaguar.)' Derek successfully ran two businesses, and still he found time to play golf occasionally for Surrey. As their marriage grew in love, and Jackie, after several years of waiting, gave birth to a boy and a girl, they felt they had somehow to share their happiness. Derek persuaded Jackie one day that they could afford to move into a bigger house so that they could foster two coloured children, to whom they had become 'aunt' and 'uncle' some time before. In the event, they ended up with the elder brother, as well.

The Brant's cosy love nest became chaos, often fun and often heart-breaking, too. The three children they were fostering all had deep problems: they were aggressive to society. Derek's and Jackie's good works had landed them in a dilemma they had not bargained for. They found, at Jackie's wits end, that human love simply was not enough. Jackie was heading for a nervous breakdown, 'but my years of training as a swimmer had taught me to keep going, on and on, even when it hurt.'

They were almost at the point of giving the foster children back to the council when Derek, one morning, went upstairs to their 5-month-old daughter, Tiffany, because she was crying, and carried her down to the lounge. Like Jackie, he had an awareness of 'a God up there', and suddenly he felt angry with that distant God because Derek could not possibly see how God could love these foster children the way Derek loved his own little baby girl. In that moment, he had an experience of God so deep 'that it was like Saul on the Damascus road.'

At different times Derek and Jackie subsequently came to sense God in a vivid, personal way. They both knew what it meant to be born again, and to be filled to overflowing with His Spirit.

Their thirst for still deeper knowledge of God led them to study for a year at 'Christ for the Nations' Bible College, in Dallas, Texas, and then for a year with a Christian community in Spain.

I know them well because they are members, with me, of the Ewell Fellowship, in Surrey. And here is what Jackie told me about the importance of that day she stood by the poolside in Cardiff with her silver medal round her neck: 'At the time, it was everything! I climbed up to receive the world's acclaim, but I had to kneel down to receive Jesus years later.

'That was the lasting crown.'

13: 'I will never leave you' (Hebrews 13:5)

When John Kilford was 14 he went with his brother, Alan, one day to see the local football team, Derby County, play Manchester United. Those were days of a legendary Derby side that included players of rare gifts, like the peerless Raich Carter and Peter Doherty, with Jack Stamps a man of teak to finish off their inspirational moves, and Dally Duncan and Tim Ward to add still more inventiveness.

They were the days, too, when the nation's appetite for their Saturday afternoon football seemed insatiable. It was long before obscene chants and raging fist-fights high on swaying terraces turned an afternoon's fun into terrifying mayhem, with police batons flaying and flick-knives lunging as warring tribes engage in pitched battle behind steel pens.

There were 43,000 people sardined into the Baseball Ground that day, and the Kilford boys, from the Derby suburb of Alvaston, were squeezed tightly down by the pitch near one of the corner flags. The crush became so suffocating that Alan fainted and had to be lifted to safety. It did not mean he had to miss the match, though: they found him a seat in the stand, and he excitedly watched it from there. Football crowds, in those times, in their flat caps and mufflers, had humour and benevolence tempering their fierce partisanship.

John Kilford never forgot that day. Even as a boy he was sensitive to atmosphere and emotion. It was not just the quality of the football, and the personality of the players, that had him wide-eyed, but the passion of the occasion. The huge crowd seemed to press right in on the footballers, and from where John stood he could hear their grunts and shouts.

'Peter! Peter! Down the line!'

'Hold it! Hold it!'

It was intoxicating stuff for a boy who lived for sport. He could play anything. Life was about getting home from school, and getting out with his mates.

In 1957 John Kilford, stockier now and blazing with eagerness, became a professional footballer himself. He had the opportunity to join Derby County, but it was Frank Broome, the manager of Notts County, a few miles away beside the River Trent, who persuaded him to sign. Two years later, John was transferred to Leeds United, and there, at Elland Road, he played alongside people like Ted Burgin, Jackie Charlton, Billy Bremner, Don Revie and Wilbur Cush. In 1961, for the first and only time in his career, he actually played at the Baseball Ground in Derby, and that was another emotional experience for him: back at the ground where he and Alan had watched Manchester United, but John out on the pitch this time, with all his family watching proudly from the stand, Alan included.

He did not have to faint before he got a clear view of the pitch that day.

Some of John's team mates, along the way, gave him the nickname 'Killer Kilford' because his tackling was so sure, but he was very much a footballer with a soft centre. When, from time to time, he was told to bite hard as he challenged for the ball (and sometimes told to be more than 'hard') he found it contrary to his instinct. His uneasiness over what genuinely went for a firm but honest tackle increased after an unfortunate incident in a reserve team game he once played for Leeds at Turf Moor, the home of Burnley Football Club. He made what he was certain was a legitimate tackle on a young opponent, and the Burnley boy's ankle broke. No amount of reassurance that it was a perfectly fair tackle could quieten the questions that searched his conscience, and for months his game suffered because of it.

Somewhere, he can recognise now, there was an influence for good working inside him, though the professional footballers he played with would almost certainly not have been aware that he had any religious convictions. John and his wife, Helen, the girl from across the road that he had been going out with since he was 15, now and again went to church on Sundays, but John can recognise today that this was largely motivated by the desire for John Kilford, the Leeds United footballer, to be seen there.

Yet as a 'teenager' in Derby, he had once made a profession of faith as a Christian, a step which, at the time, he considered both irrevocable and surprising. Surprising because his early boyhood experience of a few Christian priests had been enough to produce in most youngsters a reaction of total cynicism. He remembers seeing one much the worse for drink, yet blissfully self-assured after going to 'confession'. Another clergyman he knew as a boy was excommunicated following a scandal in the parish.

John's introduction to church attendance had hardly been with the ideal motivation. An enthusiastic new vicar had come to the local church and at once set about assembling a boys' choir. There was pocket money as a bait, and, besides, 'it meant going along with the lads', which was John's endless pleasure. So he joined, and eventually he became head choirboy.

One summer the boys from the choir were taken to a camp near Bournemouth. It deluged with rain all week, and John, who had been put in charge of one of the small tents, laid the ground sheet upside down. The tent became so soaking wet that they had to be moved into a large marquee. The sense of comradeship generated in that marquee as the rain fell, and the boys improvised their amusement, excitingly met some need in him. There was that sensitivity to 'atmosphere' again: it made John's heart swell.

So did the message that was being told to the campers all week: that there was a God so extraordinary that He loved everybody and wanted to be part of each life. One evening, before they returned home to Derby, he remembers running out of the marquee with tears of joy running down his face. He invited Jesus into his life.

John Kilford's experience just goes to show that you do not immediately begin to sprout wings when you say you have become a Christian. He believed the commitment was sincere, but within twelve months football, not God, had become his reason for living. He had become a professional, and his career dominated everything. He still went to church on Sundays, but now it was to sit at the back with the lads, whispering and giggling.

John was what the Bible calls a 'backslider'. His life as a Christian could have ended there, because God never compels us. His is a still, small, insistent voice, and we can let the noise of the world drown it. He promises, though, that he will never leave His sons and daughters, and He never left John Kilford. When he left Leeds United, he and Helen moved south, and he played non-League football. While he was at Tonbridge, Helen had their two children, first Alison then Peter. After Peter's birth, she suffered post-natal depression, and that created stresses; but there were other reasons for John's growing sense of disturbance.

'I was disenchanted by my own performances on the field. It wasn't fun, either, having to play at places like Barry and Merthyr Tydfil after Elland Road. So I decided, "That's that! I'm finishing with football." I was actually on the dole for three weeks until a friend got me a job in accountancy.

'Then one day, out with the baby in the pram, Helen met one of the curates from Tonbridge Parish Church in the street, and he started to call at our home. She began taking the children to Sunday school. I'd drive them there, then go and play cricket. I'd often be home late at night because I was working hard, but, what with one thing and another, it sometimes suited me. One of the curates, Graham Dow, would wait in the house with Helen until I did come in, and we began to talk seriously. The perseverence of Graham, John Aldis and Gordon Langrell began to tell, and eventually Helen and I went on a parish weekend in the Sussex countryside, and I re-committed my life to Christ.

'I remember saying to Graham Dow: "It's got to be 100 per cent this time. I don't want just an emotional experience." '

So he systematically thought out the foundations of his faith, and a deep desire for God welled in him now. He soon became the church youth club leader, but God had not finished with him. Within a few months his faith was to receive another momentous infusion. John and Helen went to a meeting in a private house in Tonbridge, and during the evening people prayed to receive the baptism of the Spirit. John was sure that God had already 'given me everything', but Helen was aware of new power in her life.

'Helen's experience, ' John recalls, 'was a great boost for *me*. Initially, it changed her completely. It was really remarkable. She almost couldn't wait to get the children to bed sometimes so that she could read her Bible and pray!' The two of them were now being carried forward on a wave of new faith, and they found that God began to answer their prayers. John, for instance, got a job that earned him much more money. He became a company director and was soon driving a Rover 2,000! Then, insidiously, concern began to arise over his priorities. He felt uneasy about some things he was being required to do in business. He delved deeply to discover his motives.

More and more clearly he felt that God was saying to him: 'I gave you the job. Now I'm taking it away from you!' He sensed that God had something different for him to do. He prayed: 'What is it? I'll go anywhere, do anything, just as long as I know.'

'Perhaps; he thought, 'I should become a clergyman.' The feeling would not go away. So one day he said to John Aldis: 'I think God wants me to go into the ministry.' John said: 'Forget it! If it's a call of God it won't go away. It will become more intense.' It did.

In 1975, John Kilford was ordained and began his ministry as curate at St John's, Eden Park, Beckenham, in Kent. Later, he became priest-in-charge at Sinfin Moor, in Derby. Now he is vicar of St John the Evangelist, in Penge, South London.

God had never left him. He cannot break a promise.

Harry Hughes' story is very different. Harry is the big extrovert I have mentioned before. He used to be a defender with famous clubs like Chelsea and West Bromwich Albion, but I best remember his footballing days for his part as captain in the exploits of Bournemouth back in 1957/58, the year they were the FA Cup giant-killers of Wolverhampton Wanderers and Tottenham Hotspur. Freddie Cox was their manager in those days, and one of the dodges they got up to in their Cup run was made to measure for the popular dailies.

It could hardly be called a revolutionary new strategy, more like a bit of kidology, but it appeared to be an ingredient in their success that season. What happened was this: when the opposition took a throw-in, one of the Bournemouth players, Ollie Norris, would jump and down in front of him to distract him. It seemed daft, really, and yet even the great Danny Blanchflower found it annoyingly off-putting. Harry recalls Norris giving Danny the treatment that day at Boscombe – 'and Danny might just as well have gone and sat in the stand, he was so ineffective!'

Harry has a story for every situation. He can see a laugh in almost any predicament. He is that kind of man: open, chatty, good-humoured, willing to 'live and let live'. So when, for example, the wing half Joe Brown (who later became manager at Burnley) used to pop religious tracts in his pocket while Harry was showering after training at Bournemouth, Harry just chuckled when he found them, and handed them to his wife, Joyce, when he got home. Joyce had become a Christian and attended Lansdowne Baptist Church.

He could see that Joe Brown 'had something different', and he knew he used to go out lay preaching, but Harry simply was not interested. He was happy to drive Joyce to church on Sundays, and collect her afterwards, but while she attended the service, he would watch the football in the park.

Things began to happen in Harry Hughes' life 20 years after he and Joyce married. That is a long time for a wife to wait. They had moved to Guildford, where Harry managed the local Southern League club, had his own sports shop, and assisted as a games master at a local school. By now, Joyce was running a creche and junior church at the Millmead Centre, and their own children,

Mandy and Simon, used to ask him: 'Why don't you come to church with us, Dad?'

'No. You go with your mother.'

Their repeated invitation did have its effect, though, and occasionally he relented, and joined the rest of the family in church. He found that he really enjoyed it, and when David Pawson came as pastor he and Harry became such good friends that Harry invited David to open his shop, rather than a star footballer.

His long talks with David Pawson over a period of three years began to have a profound influence. Other people, like the evangelist Eric Clark (who came into the shop to buy some squash shoes while on a three-week crusade) and the brilliant blind pianist Peter Jackson, deeply impressed Harry by what they had to say.

One evening Harry volunteered to drive Peter Jackson to Bisley Prison, where Peter was to talk to some of the prisoners. 'I thought I'd take him because I used to go there twice a week to take them for sport, and I sat and listened to what he had to say to them. He was quite fantastic. Some of the hard nuts were really touched, and so was I. I suddenly realised that night that it had been me who'd been blind all my life, not Peter.

'On our way home afterwards, Peter asked me: "How long have you been a Christian, then?" '

'I said: "Actually I'm not." '

'Peter said: "Oh, dear, we'll have to do something about this. Can we have a talk?"'

'We did – next day.' And some time later Harry was baptised in, of all places, the River Jordan, with David Pawson, whose patient and understanding ministry had been the key, conducting the baptismal service.

Several years later, at a Christians in Sport dinner in London, Harry Hughes met up again with Joe Brown, the footballer who used to leave tracts in his jacket pockets in the dressing room at Bournemouth. The smiles on their faces said everything there was to be said.

14: *T-winning for God*

It is quite possible no-one recognised it at the time, but there was obviously a hidden spark in the sixth form at Abbeydale Grange School, in Sheffield, one year not so long ago. The classroom, no doubt, was much like any other: fag-ends of chalk round the blackboard, yesterday's algebra now just indecipherable smudges where today's Elegy tells of country ploughmen, stacks of dog-eared exercise books waiting to be marked.

They probably looked a motley collection there, the spotty, the dreamy, the gigglers, the shy: incorrigibly wistful, some of them, for the adventures of the playing fields. Yet five of those contemporaries, at least, were from a hybrid strain: five grew up to be international sportsmen and women.

There was Sebastian Coe, skinny and quiet and always training. For him the world of athletics was to be thrillingly conquered: an authentic great. Then there was Philip Kidger, who became such a good badminton player, and Judith Walker, who was to excel at table tennis.

On top of that, there was Jane and Jill Powell. Jane there on the left – or is that Jill? Absolutely identical twins, mischevious and open and smiling to the world. They were both to play cricket for England. They talk of Jane (the elder by an hour) as the Derek Randall of women's cricket, and Jill as the Ian Botham. They actually played together in a full England team once: that was in 1979, against the West Indies at Steetley, in Nottinghamshire. Jane has also played left inner for the England B team at hockey: she has experienced the heady delight of walking out of the tunnel at Wembley Stadium into the shrill ecstasy of the crowd.

The tales they can tell! Hilarious ones, like all the times they pretended to be each other, and reduced their friends to total confusion. Serious ones, as well, like that hot morning in Jammu, North India, when they were due to play together in the Young England cricket team against the senior India eleven in 1981. It was half-past eight in the morning of the match when the England players looked with a mixture of concern and dismay at the condition of the outfield.

Only a month before there had been a military display on the ground, and tanks had clattered across it, leaving two-inch ruts that still had not been rolled flat. To run on it would have meant risking broken ankles, or worse. Yet they were supposed to play a Test match on it, and soon there would be 50,000 volatile spectators packing into the place, hungry for the cricket. It called for concerted action. The England players were unanimous: they could not possibly play, and Jill Powell, as captain, had to tell the officials of their decision. She did so before nine o'clock. At one o'clock it was finally decided to inform the crowd.

In their anger and frustration some hot-heads set fire to the stand, as the England girls sat beleaguered in their dressing room, their bags stacked against the door in case anyone tried to get in. Eventually they all piled into a cross between an Army truck and a Black Maria and were driven away from the ground, ducking low beneath the height of the windows for fear of being seen. It is difficult to credit such crowds, and such threat of violence, at a women's cricket match, but ask any cricketer, man or woman, who has played in India, and they will tell you stories of unforgettable sights there.

Jane and Jill Powell were always together, sharing each other's good and bad times as readily as they shared each other's clothes. They were each other's No 1 fans, especially when it came to sport. They even chose the same career, but when, at 18 years of age, they decided to go to physical education college, they agreed it would be in their best interests, to help them develop as individuals, if they enrolled at different places. Jill went to Dartford, Jane to Chelsea PE College in Eastbourne. It was the first time they had ever really been apart.

Jill had been at Dartford a year when she reached a watershed in her life. She had been setting herself one target after another in her sporting and academic life, achieving it, and then, increasingly, musing to herself: 'What next?'

She was dogged by the feeling that has nagged so many successful people: there has got to be more to life than this! The view from the top of the mountain called Worldly Acclaim was never the breathtaking fulfilment you imagined it would be. There was still a vague sense of searching. But for what? One of the girls at the college had said: 'Try Jesus!', but Jill's spontaneous reaction had been to scoff. Rather like Jane, her view of 'religious' people was that they were a bit wet. Soppy.

Throughout the following week, though, Jill could not help thinking of those words: 'Try Jesus!' She began to read a Bible. Not long after that, Jane, who was doing teaching practice at Horsham at the time, received a momentous letter from her twin in Dartford. Jane beams a toothy smile as today she recalls the surprise of the contents. 'Jill wrote to say she'd sort of found a new friend, and his name was Jesus. He was a friend who would never let her down. She'd become a Christian, and it was typical of her that she wanted to be sure I'd hear it from her first, not by way of someone else. The other thing I remember about it was that it was such a happy letter.'

Jane's reaction was sharp. 'I panicked!'

She asked her landlady: 'Have you got a Bible I could borrow for a while?' Her landlady looked so shocked that 'I think she thought I'd flipped!'

Being an hour the senior of the twins, Jane had always considered herself Jill's protector, and she borrowed the Bible because 'I wanted to check out that it was all right for Jill, being a Christian. So I sat down, and I opened the Bible at the first page, and I simply read. I wasn't very impressed with Genesis, I remember!'

At weekends the students used to return from teaching prac. to their college, and it was there that Jane's investigations led her to approach a member of the Christian Union. 'What's it all about?' she asked. She began going to meetings of the student's Christian Union, sneaking in at the back so that not too many of the girls would notice. Jane, after all, was a college sporting celebrity: she found out later that word had already got round some of the CU that she had been making enquiries about their faith, and a few of the girls had begun to pray for her. 'When I was told that, I thought, "Oh, Blimey!" '

It did not take long for Jane to make up her mind about being a Christian. She had talked it through, and she had read for herself what the Bible really had to say, not what she had always assumed it to say. There was a difference. 'Christianity', she came to the conclusion, 'was OK. And if it was OK for Jill, then it should be OK for me.'

'After one meeting of the CU I went back to one of the girls' flats, and I said I knew I had to do something about this, and she prayed with me. Immediately afterwards, I remember, we walked along the Eastbourne seafront. It was a dark November night, but I saw things that I'd never before seen in that way – the waves, the sky. Oh, you know! Then I wrote to Jill, saying I'd been checking it out, and she'd be pleased to know that I'd become a Christian, as well.'

After her four-year course at college, Jane found a job near home. She is PE teacher at the City School, in Sheffield. In fact, the very first week she was there she found some of the members of her young hockey team arguing about God. She told them she was a Christian, and what her faith meant to her. One of the girls confided in her that she and a friend had been praying for three years that a teacher would come to the school who would be a live Christian. Soon a school Christian Fellowship was started by the three of them. Eventually they began to attract as many as 30 or 40 pupils to their weekly lunchtime meetings.

Jane attends Emmanuel Church, in Waterthorpe, an ecumenical church on a new housing estate where she lives with her parents.

As for Jill her early steps as a Christian were missing the powerful thrust they might have had. For a couple of years she was without a regular church, where she might have been well taught and discipled, and when she left college in 1978 to begin a job at a Hertfordshire sports centre, Jill experienced the battle of conflicting priorities that many, many Christians have known and not all have won. That was her test of faith, and through it God became bigger and more real to her. She was to need that unbending faith, because there were times ahead that tested her ability to stand alone, if necessary. She has made abundantly clear, for example, her views on homosexuality, and she has not always been popular for doing so.

Jill is now deputy supervisor at New Court Christian School, in Finsbury Park, London.

The Powell twins have the conviction that their particular mission field is the cricket field and the hockey field. They have thought about withdrawing from the sporting arena, but their concern is that, had they taken that course, there would be two fewer witnesses to the truth that life, indeed, has more to offer than the crowd's applause and a place in the record books.

Jane succinctly sums up the sisters' shared belief in the value of Christians in sport. 'Youngsters sometimes admire sportsmen more than anyone else,' she says. 'They dream about being superstars. The girls want to be Olga Korbut. The boys want to be Kevin Keegan.'

The Powell sisters are evangelists in batting gloves and pads.

There are some notable Christians in men's cricket, as well, today, like Alan Knott. Many years ago the great C. T. Studd was well known for the strength of his faith. When the Studd family came under the influence of the American preacher, Dwight L. Moody, C.T. felt he should give away his wealth and serve God as a missionary in China. He helped to found the Worldwide Evangelization Crusade and died in the Congo in 1931. C. T. Studd was a Christian in sport long before some of us placed inverted commas round that title.

Christian sportsmen are speaking out in many parts of the world. People like Rudy Hartono, the Indonesian I suppose you can think of as the Bjorn Borg of badminton. He has been that pre-eminent. Rudy is a gentle, smiling man, who is eagerly telling all the other Indonesian badminton internationals about his faith, and the exciting change in his life.

The newest international sportsman in Britain to become a Christian is the footballer, Justin Fashanu, who, when he was transferred from Norwich City to

Nottingham Forest in the summer of 1981, cost a million pounds. Wisely, the members of Talbot Street Pentecostal Church, in Nottingham, where he belongs, sought for many months to insulate Justin against the media's prying questions, and the well-meaning but sometimes overwhelming attention of the Christian world.

Justin, after all, is big news, a big, powerful goal scorer, frank and articulate, a young man of many parts, as well. As a boy, he was a promising amateur boxer who reached national finals and was seen by some expert eyes as a future professional heavyweight fighter. Once, for a week, he acted with Sadler's Wells at the Theatre Royal, in Norwich. ('They wanted some urchins for one of their productions,' he remembers with a chuckle, 'and a local drama school recommended one or two of us. They knew I was a boy soprano in a church choir, and I'd done some television with the Norwich Boys' Choir.')

Football, though, was the career that claimed him, and Norwich City's John Bond and John Sainty nipped in to sign him when Peterborough United were not looking! At the time of writing, Justin, at 21 years of age, has already been in the full England squad for a World Cup qualifying match against Romania, won two England youth caps, twelve England under-21 caps, and made one appearance in the England B team. He is now on the books of Notts County.

In many ways, Justin did not begin life with many advantages. One of five children, he was sent to a Dr Barnardos home, then later, with his younger brother John, he was given a home with foster parents in Norfolk. He speaks of his foster Mum and Dad with moving affection. It was they who encouraged him to go to the local Church of England, though he admits that, in those days, 'I only went along for a chat and to mess about!'

All very normal! I can relate to that, and I am sure many of you can, as well.

It was in Nottingham, making his own way in the world, that the thin flame of faith flickered and then burst into life in Justin's heart. He got to wondering: where am I coming from, and where am I going? He felt that he had got where he was by his own intuition and know-how, and yet, paradoxically, he felt insecure, as well.

'Believing in a loving God is something that hasn't come hard to me,' he says significantly, 'and now I KNOW I'm a Christian! I just KNOW it!' And that certainty, in his heart, has given him a greater sense of security 'because I know there's more to life.'

Justin has been cautious about speaking of his faith too readily. On one hand he wanted people to know he is a Christian because that could encourage some of them. On the other hand, he felt wary because he sensed that he was not immediately prepared to answer some of the questions that people might put to him. He was conscious of his need for teaching, and for experience of the Christian life.

Like many new Christians, he discovered that the Devil was determined to undermine his faith while he was still a 'babe' in Christ, and Justin's trial was the much-publicised difficulty he had with the Nottingham Forest manager, Brian Clough, leading up to his transfer across the Trent to Meadow Lane. Brian Clough was extensively quoted as saying some things that would have evoked a bitter retort from many people, but Justin's unwillingness to claim 'an eye for an eye' did not go unnoticed. 'People said they couldn't understand how relaxed I was over the whole business. Well, I've got to say it was God's work. He made me feel that the issues weren't as important as all that. The Lord was a terrific help!'

Of all the things that Justin said to me when we talked, the admission that most deeply impressed me was this:

'The other players? Oh, yes, they know I'm a Christian, all right. No doubt about that. I'm not bothered about them knowing. The most difficult thing, though, is when I blow it sometimes out there on the pitch, and I know I'm not being a good witness to them.'

That had the ring of sincerity to me.

Like anyone else, Justin Fashanu may go on with God the rest of his life, or he may falter. God never takes away our free will to make our own choices. The world is ever ready to flatter and corrupt. But I know that Justin's courage, his willingness to stand up and be counted, to risk the jibes and the scoffers, his candour and his honesty will be honoured by God.

His new life could well turn out to be one of the most significant miracles that God has performed among Christians in sport, because the church needs pioneers to lead it from its middle-class cosiness into the Coronation Streets of Britain, where accents are not always pure, the colour of the skin may be different, and so may the culture.

God inhabits the praise of a steel band as much as the grand piano in the drawing room.

15: *A caring shepherd*

One nine-year-old schoolboy sitting enraptured on the grass at The Oval one summer day in 1938 watching Len Hutton, the famous England opening batsman, amass part of his record score of 364 runs, was no ordinary boy. For one thing he possessed iron loyalty to heroes and causes, as he proved one day across London, at Lord's, when he was bold enough to ask his idol, the Yorkshire and England slow left-arm bowler Hedley Verity, for his autograph as Verity strode towards the practice nets.

Verity declined, his mind on more serious things, but that schoolboy worshipper's adulation for him never waned.

For another thing, he was a boy of searching perception. As he would sit in the public stands at the nursery end at Lord's, or the sea end at Hove when he was on school holidays, he would set himself the task of identifying every fielder as soon as possible (no flashing lights on the scoreboards in those days!) and a comparison of the techniques of different batsmen gripped him in ocean-deep concentration.

No, no ordinary boy. No ordinary boy would have invented, for his own amusement, a whole county cricket championship of his own, which he played – alone –

throughout the summer after his father, a solicitor, had died and he had moved from London with mother and sister to the Sussex village of Slinfold.

The boy fantasised a season's fixture list, with seventeen counties playing each other, and he was each batsman, in turn, on every side. His pitch was a patch of grass outside the back door. His wicket was the door of the coal shed. He would throw a tennis ball at the door, left-handed as he is, and play a shot as it rebounded. Not just any shot, either. If that day's match was Middlesex against Derbyshire, and if he was Compton batting, he would never hit the ball in the air but cover-drive and late-cut and hook. If he was Hammond, he would not allow himself to hook. The point was, he had to make his runs the way the stars of the day would have made them.

Certainly no ordinary boy. His name was David Sheppard.

His prep. school headmaster, back in 1939 had some slight sense of the boy's gift when he observed, with what proved to be not only monumental under-statement but also squint vision: 'Young Sheppard, if I am not very much mistaken, will one day cause a great many batsmen a great deal of trouble with his left-arm slows.'

In fact, his boyhood ambition was to be a slow left-arm bowler, hence his adulation of Verity. His method of turning the ball in those innocent days was entirely homespun (that seems to be the right word!). It was an art he lost as he came into knowledge of technique. He amusingly recalls what happened in his book, 'Parson's Pitch': 'I started reading books and learning how to spin the ball properly, and I have never been able to spin the ball, off-breaks or leg-breaks, from that day to this.'

Cricket was David's absorbing interest. Throughout the summer there were the county scores to assimilate in the daily papers, a whole library shelf of books on the game's great exponents, early-morning paradise of 'wireless' commentaries of Test matches in far-off places like Australia. Oh, actually to be there one day! He had other heroes, besides Hedley Verity: men like the imposing Wally Hammond, of England, and Don Bradman, of Australia. He remembers to this day a news-vendor's placard in King's Road, Chelsea, declaring to the world: 'BRADMAN FAILS AGAIN.' Bradman had indeed failed: only 82 runs!

He eagerly enlisted family involvement in his garden games – not the serious stuff of his one-man county championship against the coal shed, you understand, but in 'friendly' matches his mother was what he describes as a 'faithful, steady underarm bowler'. His sister used to bowl fast rounders, which meant that after about every other delivery from her, play had to be interrupted while they searched for the ball in the prickly hedge.

As night followed day, David Sheppard's young life broke upon a dawn of international cricket. He played 22 Test matches for England as an opening batsman. His first England match was in 1950, the last Test in the series that year against the West Indies, and held at The Oval. One of the established firm of England openers, Cyril Washbrook, was injured, so David was called up to take his place, to share the drama of a pitched battle against giant cricketing figures like Worrell, Walcott and Weekes, Ramadhin and Valentine – legends almost. His final Test for England was in 1963, against New Zealand in Christchurch. His quality and resolution were so respected that the England selectors even recalled him for a tour of Australia at a time when he had been out of day-to-day first-class cricket for seven years.

He played cricket for Cambridge University and for Sussex. His first match for Sussex was in 1947. It was against Leicestershire in Hastings. He was 18 years old, and he was out first ball! They had told him the only bowler he had to worry about in the Leicestershire side was Walsh, but the only ball he received in that first innings was from Jackson, and they had not mentioned him. It was an in-swinger, and he was out leg before wicket. In Sussex's second innings, David scored two runs before he was caught at the wicket. He had still not received a ball from Walsh.

From that inauspicious beginning, he matured into a player to become synonymous with names like Compton and Bailey and Bedser, Hutton, Lindwall and Miller.

He still feels intensely a part of Sussex cricket. He told me he can say any day in the summer what Sussex have done that day. 'I still feel it.' Sussex had helped him love cricket in a new dimension. 'In big cricket,' he has written, 'there are many occasions, when the going is tough, when you cannot truthfully say, "I'm enjoying myself." I think the enjoyment is of the whole experience of facing a challenge of skill and nerve in the fellowship of a good team which pulls together.'

You may think that says something about the experience of life itself.

Let's, though, consider the anatomy of the David Sheppard who went up to Trinity Hall in Cambridge. Cricket had become an absorbing interest to him, but not a consuming one. His vision, already, was a good deal broader than that of most back-garden tyros dreaming of England centuries and hat-tricks. Wisden had not been his only reading, by any means: he had ranged from the lightest school stories to 'War and Peace', to Churchill's 'Marlborough', to Galsworthy, Thackeray and Jane Austen. He had developed a passion for classical music, as well, especially Beethoven, and he often used to go to concerts, or opera, or ballet with his mother: the technique of Margot Fonteyn and Robert Helpmann had inspired him. It was their unhurriedness: the same lack of flurry of the great cricketers he so admired.

He had sung at Sherborne School, in Dorset, when he was a pupil there. He had even sung soprano solo in Sherborne Abbey. And now here he was arriving at Cambridge, famous seat of learning, to read history for two years and law in his third year. His intention was to become a Barrister-at-Law.

People would have said of the student Sheppard that he was 'a decent chap.'

Christian ideas of worship and morality had been impressed on him strongly as a boy. He went to church fairly regularly and was confirmed. 'I believed strongly,' he wrote in 'Parson's Pitch', 'that I should try to follow Christ's example.' But as he grew up and moved on in his life there was a growing dissatisfaction as, in the real business of day-to-day living, mixing with people of different religious faith or none at all, fine idealism seemed without much hope to support it. He experienced the sense that God was 'away in the distance'. Prayer seemed like 'looking up to a cloudy sky.' He found himself praying sincerely mostly when he was up against some crisis or personal failure.

'The way things seemed to me was that I was already on the road and must struggle on, becoming a little more religious until one day, perhaps, I might arrive.'

The idea that he might not be on the road at all, he admits, never occurred to him at the time.

He had been taught, in a loving and secure home, how to behave 'naturally', without striving to impress others. He had been taught, at school, to be reliable: a man of his word. He had learned a tradition of service, of doing things for others, 'which I regard as the greatest part of what is good in public school education.' In students' lodgings at Cambridge they talked fervently of many things, the 'meaning of life', politics, religion, but they usually avoided actually mentioning the name 'Jesus'. 'That was too personal and embarrassing by far.

It had always been like that in my life. We could discuss good neighbourliness, or the needs of the poor; we could talk about the new rector's habits, about criticisms of the Bible, or about religious fanatics. But somehow it seemed almost indecent to speak about God and Christ, and I doubt if I had heard anyone speak simply of trust in God since my Mother had talked to me as a child.'

As I say, David was a thoroughly decent chap, well mannered, intelligent, secure, talented, not wanting to 'do the other fellow down.' In other words, he was the archetypal English middle-class 'good, clean young man'.

He was the most difficult species of all, in my limited experience, to convince of a need of personal forgiveness by God and a new life infused by the Holy Spirit. A broken man can see that need, as the debris of a life of crime or self-will lays scattered round him. A bereaved man can see it, as he reaches out in his unutterable loneliness. A dying man can see it, as the last moments ebb from his life. Sometimes an inspired man can see it as he drinks in the breath-taking beauty of a landscape or a symphony, or holds his own child snugly in his arms for the first time, sensing his complete inadequacy to appreciate the miracle of creation.

But a 'jolly good fellow' – how do you deal with him?

How do you penetrate that armour-plating of uprightness, self-sufficiency, and, above all, pride? What tells a man who has everything that he has nothing *of his own*? How do you tell one of England's most skilful young cricketers, a moderate, modest, intelligent and painstaking student cosseted throughout his young life by the cosiness of the middle-class?

Well, in the case of David Sheppard it all began on a squash court. (It did not, really, of course. As any experience Christian will know it began in somebody's prayerful concern for him.) John Collins, then a theological student at Ridley Hall, Cambridge, now vicar of Holy Trinity, Brompton, played David at squash one day, and then they went off to relax together over a cup of tea. There was a mission taking place at the university, and John invited David to go along with him one evening.

When David had first arrived at Trinity Hall he had torn up all the literature that had been sent to him by various Christian groups because he was determined not to be browbeaten, but he agreed to go along with John Collins on this occasion, and the two of them sat together in the body of Great St Mary's Church. The speaker was an American, Dr Donald Barnhouse. His style was aggressive – 'in a way, made for someone like me,' David remembers. 'His target was very much conventional religion. I had always thought that I was on the road, but he convinced me that I wasn't.'

One great truth got through David's defences. He had been able to persuade himself, when he compared his life with others, that he was as good as most and better than some. But, listening to Dr Barnhouse, he realised that he was facing the judgement of God Himself, that he was to be judged by God's standards, not society's, and that he desperately needed to be forgiven.

He realised too, that sin could not be limited to a few outward blemishes that people could see ('We have done those things that we ought not to have done,' as the confessional puts it), but just as much included 'the things we have left undone that we ought to have done.' Most of all, it tore him to his heart that he needed to be forgiven because he had turned his back on God, gone his own way.

In 'Parson's Pitch', David recalls: 'Again and again Barnhouse returned to his great theme that no man can climb up to God by his own efforts to be kind, neighbourly or religious. Only by the totally unreserved love and grace of Jesus Christ can anyone be accepted. I believe this was also the great theme of the Apostles, "For it is by His grace you are saved, through trusting Him; it is not your own doing. It is God's gift, not a reward for work done. There is nothing for anyone to boast of." '

David now listened with new urgency to what John Collins told him about Jesus, and how He had taken everyone's place on the cross that dreadful, mighty day a Calvary. If he could 'accept Christ' in real faith it would be an end to 'doing his best and hoping he'd get there one day' and the start of a new life in which he could, with honesty, say, 'I believe in the forgiveness of sins.'

He said to John Collins: 'Yes, that would be wonderful, but it wouldn't be any good. I should be just the same person, sand I should never be able to keep it up.' John showed him that, it is true, we all let God down; that the Christian never claims to be someone who has achieved righteousness, but somebody who knows he is sinful and accepts God's undeserved forgiveness over and over again.

He also helped him see that if you sincerely ask Jesus Christ to come into your life, you will never be quite the same again. A new force will have been let loose in your life.

That evening, at Cambridge, David heard a verse from the Bible for the first time that seemed to make the whole thing clear to him: 'Here I stand knocking at the door; if anyone hears My voice and opens the door, I will come in and sit down to supper with him and he with me.'

That made it quite plain to David. Either Christ was outside the door of his life, or He was inside. There was no acceptable in-between. David knew then that he had never sincerely asked Jesus to enter his life and take charge of it. He walked back to his rooms at Trinity

Hall late that night, convinced that it was more important than anything else in the world – more important than his cricket, more important than his studies and his ambition to become a Barrister-at-Law – that he should become right with God.

'I knelt in my bedroom, and, praying in my own words, I asked Christ to come into my life, to forgive me, and to be my Friend and Master. Then I prayed something like this, "Lord, I don't know where this is going to take me, but I'm willing to go with you. Please make me willing." ' The 'please make me willing' was an honest plea because he was afraid that he might not feel the same when he woke up next morning.

'It was,' he says, 'as if a jumble of loose threads suddenly fitted into place.' His conversion had been in one night, but all the preceding years of Christian background had somehow helped to prepare him for it. There was no magic change of his feelings, or his actions, after he prayed that prayer, but as he began to move into relationships with other Christians, together trying to work out the friendship of Christ every day, so he began to grow.

He began to ponder on whether God wanted him to continue to spend so much time playing cricket. He wondered what Jesus's own attitude would be. He read in the Bible how Jesus worked with His hands till He was thirty years old, and that He came to do His Father's will not on the sidewalks of life, but in the middle of the world of men. 'I believe,' wrote David, 'that today He wants His followers in the middle of every walk of life, and I am persuaded that it was His will for me to give some years to playing cricket.'

Eventually, though, in 1955, he was ordained in St Paul's Cathedral. His thought, at that time, was that he might become a chaplain in a public school, but between 1955 and 1957, when he was curate at St Mary's,

Islington, in London, he underwent what he refers to as his 'second conversion.' The years he spent in Islington he began to feel deeply disturbed about working-class people. He realised how huge was the gap between working-class people and the churches of all denominations. 'I was plunged into a different culture,' he told me, 'and all my pre-suppositions had to be questioned.'

David Sheppard expressed in action his concern for less privileged people during the years he was warden of the Mayflower Family Centre in London's East End, in Canning Town, and later when he became Bishop of Woolwich.

Since 1975 he has been Bishop of Liverpool. He has hurt for the problems that spilled over in his very patch – in Toxteth. And now he has written movingly of the unequal burden of unemployment and disadvantage in society in his book, *Bias to the Poor*.

16: *Hot potatoes for a rugger man*

You have got this far, but perhaps there is still some stubborn blockage to you taking a step in faith. People offer the most surprising objections to making a fresh start: a professional footballer once insisted that his personal Beecher's Brook (if you will excuse the mixed metaphor) was that he felt he would have to give up his customary eight pints of beer on a Saturday night if he became a Christian.

Because your stumbling blocks may be of more substance than that, it will take a robust man – robust physically, mentally and spiritually – to handle some of the hot potatoes you may be wanting to toss.

I asked Alan Godson to do this handling. He was a Cambridge rugby Blue; he played, also, for Lancashire, Manchester, Bristol and Harlequins, not to mention Bill Beaumont's old club, Fylde.

Alan has another qualification to fit him for this particular task in a book about sporting people: he is chairman of 'Christians in Sport'.

He could hardly have been better named: Godson – son of God. So for this chapter I pass to him, and to the Holy Spirit.

Question – What about the millions of people in the forests of Africa and the mountains of Bengal, for example, who have never heard the Christian Gospel? Are you saying they are bound for hell?

First of all, the Gospel is God's Good News, that He really does care for everyone, and His outreach is everywhere. Essentially He is a God who is just, someone in whose character we can completely trust. What He does, therefore, with those who have never heard of Jesus Christ will be utterly fair. We don't have the whole story as to how God deals with people such as these. 'There are secrets that the Lord God has not revealed to us' (Deut 29:29). We must concentrate on what He *has* shown us. No-one who has not heard of Jesus Christ will be condemned for rejecting Him, only for rejecting his own moral standard, high or low. In other words, we each have our own understanding of how we should act and what we should be. Paul, in Romans 2, is very clear that everyone is aware of doing wrong: 'He will punish the heathen when they sin, even though they never had God's written laws, for down in their hearts they know right from wrong.'
But, really, these questions are only side-tracks for the one who doesn't *want* to find the truth.

Question – What about people of other religions – Muslims and Hindus and Buddhists – don't they all worship the same God as a Christian, but under another name?

Really we're asking, Is Jesus the only way to God? You know, we can be sincere and wrong. We can have deep faith, but it can't make it true. For faith is only as valid as the object in which it is placed. Believing

141

doesn't make somethimg true. Nor does unbelief make it a lie.

For me, the big question we all have to ask about the Christian message is never asked, i.e. Is it really true? If it is, we are fools not to follow Christ.

Recently, after speaking in a university, I was taken away by a bunch of Iranians to a special room, and, after entering, the door was locked behind me. I had no need to fear: they just did not want to be interrupted. For the first time in their lives, they said that they had heard someone speak who seemed to believe that Jesus Christ was still alive, and they wanted to find out. You see, maybe morally and ethically there isn't too much difference between Islam and Christianity, but they absolutely differ on the question: Who is Jesus Christ? Islam denies that Jesus is the son of God, that He died on the cross, and rose from the dead. The Christian points to the cross on which Jesus died for our sin, and to His glorious resurrection. Both can't be right. If the Christian claim is false, then our faith would be worthless.

When a Christian is accused of being arrogant about his belief, it is only because we are saying what Jesus has said. We must make our stand on what He has said, not on our own definitions. If He *is* God, He must be the only answer. We can't adjust the truth for the convenience of anyone, for this truth has been revealed. It is not our invention. God stepped into history in Jesus Christ.

A Hindu has many gods; a Buddhist has no god. What about you?

Question – If there really is a loving God, how can he stand by and watch as innocent children die from agonising sickness and from man's brutality?

If deep down some instinct did not tell you that there

is a loving God, you would not even raise this question. And we must confess a partial ignorance here. The origin of evil is not fully revealed. We are told, however, that planet Earth was created perfect, but that man was free to obey or disobey God. Evil came through man's disobedience. Man's actions are never limited to himself but always affect others.

Because God's law was broken, evil permeates the planet Earth. God, of course, is much bigger than this: he made the whole universe. 'Why doesn't God get rid of evil?' goes up the cry! Why doesn't God get rid of you and me! If midnight was the hour at which God decreed the defeat of evil, would any of us be around to celebrate? What we can say, however, is that God has done more than enough to combat the problem of evil. He not only entered history in Jesus, but died to solve the problem. Everyone who willingly receives His gift of loving forgiveness is accepted in Him. C. S. Lewis, who was a professor of English as well as Christ when I was in Cambridge, suggested that 'it was idle to speculate about the origin of evil. The problem we all face is the fact of evil.'

There is only one solution that God has given us: Jesus Christ. At the heart of all suffering is the innocent son of God. If we cry out, He is in total agony, until He overcomes.

Question – You surely don't expect people to take the Bible literally, do you?

Those people who ask this question have hardly read the Bible at all, and can rarely think of where the errors might lie. Of all the problems known to man, there are few that the Bible hasn't largely solved. Evolution is only a problem when it leads to an atheistic position. Not too many people believe that the universe was created by accident. Maybe God did, indeed, use evolutionary processes. I am sure Charles Darwin, who was a member of my old college – Christ's Cambridge – did not die an unbeliever.

Yes, the Bible is truly God's revelation to man, displaying His concern and purpose for the highest part of His creation – you and me. And even Jesus regarded the Old Testament as authoritative writ for Him. It is a book of divine origin, and no book has been so carefully studied. It is the world's best-seller, God's word in the language of men.

Question – If you believe in a personal God, do you believe in a personal devil, as well?

Yes, I really do. Twentieth-century man has ably demonstrated that even he, with all his knowledge, cannot act so stupidly without tremendous encouragement. This comes from the devil himself, who, because he is on a course of self-destruction, seeks the world's destruction. Satan is another of his names, which means the 'accuser of men' – and women, too! He seeks avidly our destruction, and pulls us down at every opportunity. But though his power is strictly limited, it is only with God's help that we can overcome and live true to ourselves and to our Maker. A master of disguise, the devil should be taken seriously. All our appetites he accentuates until they exceed their worth. For example, gluttony makes food an idol when it should only satisfy. Sex becomes a goddess to be worshipped at our peril. Knowledge becomes an end in itself, instead of leading us to God. Pride props up our egoism and takes away our personal dignity as we recognise no-one higher than ourselves. The devil is the past master at causing men to doubt that God has a loving plan for the whole of His creation. The devil does believe in God, however, and the Bible, and trembles in His company.

144

Question – Do you seriously believe there's a heaven and a hell waiting for us when we die?

Yes I do. Most people think of Jesus as being the world's greatest lover. Most, however, forget that He always told the truth, as well. If He invites us to join Him as a true son or daughter of our heavenly Father, He must also leave us free to respond. God never insists that we should join Him in heaven. Conversely, He never insists that He should leave us in hell. Heaven I define as being in God's presence after death. Hell is the experience of forsaking God, which ends in God-forsakenness.

Jesus says in John's Gospel, chapter 3, verses 17 and 18: 'God did not send His son into the world to condemn it but to save it. There is no eternal doom awaiting those who trust Him to save them. But those who do not trust Him have already been tried and condemned for not believing in the only son of God.' The Christian challenge is essentially positive: 'Do this and you will live.' 'Come to me,' says Jesus, 'and I will strengthen you.' He does not insist that we come, and He loves us enough to let us go. Not many people, when I ask them would they like to go to heaven, say No. Sadly, not so many people say Yes to Jesus *now*. It's a mystery I have not yet solved!

Question – I've got a loving marriage, happy children, a sound job, and I have confidence in my own good sense. Why on earth do I need to bother with God?

Why on earth not? Is it wrong to say Thank You to the giver of all good gifts? And as love is the supreme gift of the supreme giver, why not recognise the source of your good fortune? Who did you thank after the birth of your first baby? I recall a late-night phone call when a woman asked me what had I done to her husband? 'What have I done to your husband?' I asked. 'Well,' she said, 'he loves me now more than he has ever done.' I enquired: 'Is that a complaint?' Her fear was that she was being pushed out, and that her husband didn't need her love any more. The Bible quickly answers this dilemma. 1 John Chapter 4, verse 19, following: 'We love because God first loved us. If someone says he loves God but hates his brother, he is a liar. For he cannot love God, whom he has not seen, if he does not love his brother, whom he has seen. The command that Christ has given us is this: Whoever loves God must love his brother also.'

If you love God, you will not love others less but even more, because your commitment does not depend upon your feelings any more. For love is not sentimental: it really has bite. It is not a commodity bought and sold: it is God's gift to men. Treasure it. Fight for it. Be eternally grateful!

Question – You can't prove that Jesus exists. Until you can, why should I pin my faith on somebody who could turn out to be a myth?

If curiosity killed the cat, it also makes men live. We were born to ask questions. Maybe the biggest question we will ever ask is: What am I living for? I would say that only God, speaking through Jesus Christ, His down-to-earth man, has given us an adequate answer. If we cannot trust the word of Jesus, whose word can we trust? If His character, as most men accept it, is likely to betray us, then why should we trust anyone else? As the proof of the pudding is in the eating, so it is only when we do what God asks of us that we will know that He is there, and can become more real to us than even our nearest and dearest. Myths have a way of being out of date. Jesus is always our contemporary. If you are to be a modern man, you need to

step out in faith with Him. He makes all the difference. He puts a flavour into life that can bring satisfac-
tion, whatever our situation.

After all, truth doesn't change with circumstances.
No-one else can take away from you the joy of finding
out that God loves you. Make sure that no-one, and
nothing, robs you of making this discovery. Choose
life! And live it to the full.

Question – OK. I believe in God, but I don't interfere
with other people, and I don't want them to interfere in
my life. History is littered with cruel wars perpetrated
in the name of religion, because people want to enforce
their religious beliefs on others. Why can't I keep my
religion to myself?

The word 'religion' tends to describe the externals of
what men believe is the way to live. *Religio* is a Latin
word which has, among other meanings, that of being
'connected'. We are connected to our families, our
jobs, the things we'll do and the things we won't; but
so few are connected to Christ in a way that is personal
and life-giving. You cannot follow His teaching
without the encouragement of His powerful presence
in your life. This is the burden that most people are
under: of doing the best they can – and still falling
short of their own standard. This develops the great
enemy of being at one with God (righteousness): that
enemy is self-righteousness. In other words, man,
unaided, imposing his standards on others. The heart
of the Christian message is forgiveness, man recognising his failure to be true to God and asking for restora-
tion, having recognised the price God has to pay for
this: his own son's death.

Wars like those in Ulster and the Middle East, which
some people say are religious wars, are nothing of the

kind. They are wars of false religion. This is certainly so in Ulster, where people claim to be Christians.

If God's call is to respect one another as equal before Him, the call of Jesus goes beyond this to even loving one's enemies. Only the revolution of love can change the situation in Northern Ireland, where unjust men seek the cause of justice without themselves fulfilling it. Who would want a man of hate to reign over them? However, it must be said of a country where 80 per cent of the population has a church attachment that something has gone wrong somewhere. No-one who kills in a cowardly and indiscriminate way can claim God's backing to his cause. There is no room for murderers in the Kingdom of Heaven.

By all means keep to ourselves the religion of death, but the Christian message is of the life-giver who loves to do what is good and comes from God.

We seem to be short on sharing the truth of a God who loves us, to whom we are personally and nationally accountable.

As for keeping your faith to yourself, if it is God's truth you are seeking to conceal from any man, you are actually stealing his life from God and will be held responsible. 'Go into all the world and share my Good News, and teach people my ways,' said Jesus to all those who are willing to learn from Him and obey Him.

John Chrysostom (a fourth-century bishop who played central defender for Constantinople!) said: 'I cannot believe in the salvation of any man who does not work towards his neighbour's salvation.'

Question – Some of the finest-living people I know don't believe in God. Some of the biggest hypocrites I know call themselves Christians. How do you answer that?

I expect only God can answer this question. For one

148

day we will all know the truth, and the truth that sought to set us free. It is sad for me to find anyone who is a friend of mine not yet being a friend of God's. It is a constant pain to me that this should ever be so. But one of the things that helped me to come to a true relationship with God was my understanding of the way He honoured me in recognising Him. Alan Godson could have turned down God's offer of His life and friendship, and, recognising this, it showed me where the dignity of any man is truly to be found. God does not insist on His rightful place in our life. He leaves us to say Yes or No to His invitation. 'Come to me.'

If fine people have developed into men and women worth knowing, most often they uphold God's standard unconsciously but fail to recognise the source of their inspiration. A self-made man, however, in the long run, is a selfish man, because he has not thanked God for his gifts in life and has failed to recognise Jesus Christ as someone who lived and died for truth and lives on, still.

A hypocrite is someone who pretends to be what he is not – and maybe man's greatest enemy in keeping others away from God. 'By their fruits you shall know them,' says the Scripture. They would be a lot fewer if, more often, they were challenged to put their actions where their mouth is. Perhaps, sadly, the reason for their existence is that we treat too lightly the honour of being called 'Christians' – both those who believe and those who do not.

Question – I once made a Christian commitment, but after the honeymoon period I found myself lapsing into the old bad habits of attitude and self-will. What is the point of beginning again?

Well, after any honeymoon we have to come back to

earth with all its responsibilities. Like any relationship, our relationship with God must develop. Otherwise it begins to fade away. Love begets love, and so we grow together, and life becomes richer. But life is a challenge, and it is often in the hard times that our characters are best formed. Relationships have to do with will, and loving somebody is doing what needs to be done.

It is not a question of how we feel at the time. It is an attitude of mind, made constant by practice. We can all make mistakes. We can all ask for forgiveness. Just as our first forgiveness, when we recognised God's generosity to us in accepting us as we were, was a gift of grace, so our subsequent failures are forgiven when asked for, because He does not change His mind about us. He helps us to change our mind, and our lives. He is the great encourager.

When Jesus asked His disciples if they were going to forsake Him, as other men were, their reply was loud and clear: 'Lord, to whom shall we go? You have the words of eternal life.' Having found life, don't lose it. Keep it – and give it away.

Question – You may think this one too trivial to answer, but it really is my hang-up. I am a young, active sportsman. I love the whole scene of sport, and part of that scene, would you believe, is my sex life on a Saturday night after the match, when the girls arrive. If I became a Christian, all that would have to end, wouldn't it?

Far from thinking your question is unimportant, it is a most vital part of anyone's life. Under control, sex is one of God's greatest gifts. Out of control, it can be disastrous.

I expect the question that everyone is asking is: Will I have to give up the good time for God's time? I would make one powerful plea here: a man's relationship with God can overcome any situation that is handed over to Him. We often say: 'I know I couldn't change in that area'; but we say it without knowing the power of God to help us to change. Sadly, many people have to play the image game – what they think people expect them to be. The art of living is about a good relationship, which takes a lifetime of work to maintain.

When you find a good girl, don't treat her as a toy. Cherish her as a lifelong companion.

Our sexual appetite needs to be under control to enjoy it to the fullest. Miscellaneous women produce miscellaneous men, and so often men think only women have to carry the can. We can only give ourselves away.

Maybe today we have lost the gift of friendship, when we value someone for what they are rather than for what they can give us. If you love someone enough to want to go to bed with her, marry the girl!

17: *On your marks!*

So what is this little book trying to say?

Well, let me say at once that I am not in the least apologetic about the fact that it is not profoundly woven with margin references to classical scholars, translations in Hebrew and Greek and deep explorations into metaphysics. That is the way for others, much more gifted in scholarship, who rightly use their God-given intellectual inquisitiveness to search great mysteries.

I recently gave a friend a simple paperback of fundamental Christian belief, written by a man whom God has used spectacularly in evangelism, and my friend later thanked me generously for the gift, which he had found readable but, I gathered, a bit upper-sixth in its simplistic approach. He is an erudite man himself, with feeling for our language, and a hunger for looking below the surface, but I sometimes fear that people like him may miss the simple truth of Jesus because they are listening for a symphony when it is a penny-whistle tune to be heard.

What kind of Gospel is it if only great minds can perceive it?

Don't forget that Paul wrote: 'The Kingdom of God is not a matter of words but of power' (1 Cor 4). And Jesus himself said (Mark 10:15): 'I assure you that whoever does not receive the Kingdom of God like a child will never enter it.'

This book, then, is an attempt to tell, from my own and other people's experience, a simple truth, and then to encourage you to decide for yourselves. God wants you to decide. We know that because the Bible tells us so. Jesus said: 'Anyone who is not for me is really against me . . .' (Matthew 12:30). And God, who is also Jesus, said: 'I know that you are neither cold nor hot. How I wish you were either one or the other! But because you are lukewarm, neither hot nor cold, I am going to spit you out of my mouth! (Revelation 3:15–16).

If, through the years, you have honestly considered the claims of the historical Jesus, and you have come to the conviction that either He was a myth or merely a wise prophet, then respect should say 'So be it', and one would assume that you would logically not want a Christian burial for yourself when the end comes to your life. Likewise you would be consistent in not, for example, marrying in a church.

On the other hand, if you know in your heart that you are merely 'playing the field', as sporting men say, 'hedging your bets', then why wait till tragedy strikes, or you are on your death-bed, to seek God? Why not find out who Jesus *really* is, not who you vaguely suppose Him to be?

Are you seriously so afraid of what your family and friends might think that you are going to put off till the last minute of your life to decide, once and for all, exactly where you stand on the greatest issue there is for any man or woman to resolve? Isn't that cowardice?

You may have been intimidated by 'churchiness', or turned off by Sunday Christians whose Monday-morning lives deny the claims they make. It may be that you 'know you couldn't possibly live up to it'. Or your steely pride. Whatever the reason, the answer is the same:

go to a bookshop and buy youself a Bible, in modern translation (the Good News Bible, for example, or the New International version). Then read carefully the New Testament, and discover the true nature of Jesus, the way of life He propounded, the unique claims He made for himself, most notably 'I am the way, the truth and the life; no-one goes to the Father except by me' (John 14:6).

Charlatan? Or nut?

Or the only son of God?

You have to make up your mind on the word of the Bible. No-one can *prove* Jesus to you. And as for the impossibility of 'living up to it', the Bible will provide an answer to that, too. You will find in Ephesians 2, verse 8: 'For it is by God's grace that you have been saved through faith. It is not the result of your own efforts, but God's gift.'

So it is all about faith, then: all about BELIEVING. And if you find that, no matter all the hang-ups and reservations you have, you really do believe that Jesus was the only son of God, that He died on the cross, that He came back from the dead, that when He sent his Holy Spirit men were immediately transformed, and that He is coming again – for that is what the Bible says – then the next step is both amazingly simple and incredibly hard.

You have simply to ask God to come into your heart, and then accept IN FAITH that, because He is God and cannot tell a lie or break a promise, He comes at that very moment, to begin a supernatural work of new birth.

You have the Bible's word on that. Jesus said: 'Ask, and you will receive . . . for EVERYONE who asks will receive' (Matthew 7:7–8). And God said: 'I stand at the door and knock; if anyone hears my voice and opens the door, I will come into his house and eat with him, and he will eat with me' (Revelation 3:20).

In other words, we have to make a positive act: we have to ask, or knock. Then God always answers, if he sees into the heart of the person asking and recognises his sincerity. Next, having taken that step, the New Testament call is insistent. As Peter declared on the Day of Pentecost: 'Each one of you must turn away from his sins and be baptized in the name of Jesus Christ, so that your sins will be forgiven; and you will receive God's gift, the Holy Spirit' (Acts 2:38).

For you to be obedient in the act of baptism, obviously you will have to be in contact with a Christian church. That should not be difficult. Look round you and find a Christian you feel you really can trust. He will welcome your enquiry and want you to meet his friends. The rest will follow.

This book, then, is an introduction to A Whole New Ball Game. You will only know whether it is for you when you begin seriously to play it. It is the only game there is where the score never changes.

Love-all.

The love of God, received in men's hearts through the agency of the Holy Spirit, is what makes the Christian's life the radical alternative to a world system which, as anyone can see, is frighteningly on course for self-destruction. Do you feel utterly powerless as the nuclear arms race continues to generate more than enough force to blow us all to smithereens? Isn't it a prospect so horrendous that many of us simply refuse to think about it? Isn't that why we live in a world of fatalism and cynicism?

Aren't you terrified by the lack of moral calibre of the politicians with their fingers on the button? Isn't there a voice inside you wanting to scream out: 'But what can *I* do about it?'

Aren't you hurting inside at the corruption you see almost everywhere you go about your daily round? Don't you ask for the broken relationships, the lack of trust, the lack of caring?

So much for higher education, for the miracles of modern communication, for the age of the cathode ray and the microchip. So much for civilisation!

'But what can *I* do about it?'

There is no social philosophy, no political creed that can change men at the point where it all begins: in our hearts. Only a supernatural act of God can do that.

You don't believe that? Well, what other power could possibly have brought about an astonishing meeting in a Chicago room not so long ago? Three men came together that day, united by an infusion of love so overwhelming that their lives had been turned in completely different directions. One of those men was Eldridge Cleaver, once a Marxist Black Panther, who had been seen by millions on American television shouting: 'Kill the pigs! Rape the white women!' He had fled, after a gun battle with the police, to Cuba, China and the Soviet Union. Then he had become a Christian, volunteered himself to the police, and was jailed.

The second man in the room that day was Tommy Tarrants, former Ku Klux Klansman, once sentenced to 30 years in jail for terrorism against black people, but who had since turned over his life to Christ.

The third man was the one who told this extraordinary story in his moving book, *Life Sentence*. He is Charles Colson, once despised as President Nixon's hatchet man, imprisoned for his part in the Watergate scandal, now devoting his life to a Christian ministry to prisons.

If you think you can't be changed, just think what happened to them.

In human terms, it is an impossible task trying to alter the course of the world, but at least you can do something about one person.

Yourself.

Other Marshalls Paperbacks

FROM PRISON TO PULPIT

Vic Jackopson

'Father died when he was a year old.
Mother deserted.
Family broken up.
Failed fostering experiment.
Above average intelligence.
One more chance.'

Vic was used to probation officers pleading his case in court. He had learnt to take care of himself early on in the orphanage, but years of fighting, stealing and burgling had brought him to the end of the line.

'God, if you are there, you've got ten days to change my life and if you haven't done it by then you've copped it.'

Vic prayed, God acted. It wasn't always easy from then on, but living by the grace of God rather than by his own fists Vic found a new inner strength and security. Instead of taking from others he now teaches and lives the new life Christ brings into the hearts of men and women.

LOVE IN 'BOMB CITY'

Ben Forde with Chris Spencer

Ben Forde, a Belfast CID detective, shares from his personal experience his conviction that amid the sectarian hatred there is a powerful force of love at work—a love which is bringing forgiveness and healing in a province notorious for its bitterness and division.

He also discusses Northern Ireland from the wider perspective of God's sovereign plan, seeking to make sense of the suffering with which he comes into contact almost every day in the course of his work. He asks: Has God forsaken Northern Ireland? Is he passing judgment on the sins of the people? Or is he actively preparing Ulster for a specific role in future world events? And what of the terrorism? Will the troubles in Northern Ireland ever end? What is the real purpose behind the violence? And how can countries like Britain and America, where terrorism is only just beginning to rear its ugly head, benefit from the painful experiences of Northern Ireland?

Love in 'Bomb City' provides some stimulating answers.

WHERE CHRIST IS STILL TORTURED

Richard Wurmbrand

'Except for the Bible, nothing has shaken me like Wurmbrand.' *Tortured for Christ*. 'It is the message of the century—Even more: it is the most powerful *Acts of the Martyrs* since the persecution of Christians by Nero.'

Kurt Koch

In this book Richard Wurmbrand brings the story up to date. Persecution continues to tighten its grip on infant Christian Churches in lands ruled by atheists and tyrants. It is only the power of the Holy Spirit which enables them to survive and flourish in the face of discrimination, oppression, torture and murder. What is the response of the cossetted Western church? Does it understand what is happening? Satanic forces are working to stifle Christian witness in the world today, and Christians in the West need to be able to recognize and fight their enemy.

MY ROUGH DIAMOND

Doris Lemon with Anne Tyler

'Not all women have husbands who turn out to be viciously tempered, drunkards, or even convicts—but some women do. It can be a nightmare to be married to such a man: the isolation of it, the shame, the loneliness you feel. And fear! Fear for yourself, for the children. How do you cope? Where do you get the stamina and endurance from?

I've written this book so as to share with you my experiences—and the lessons I learned from them—and to tell you that God is able to make all the difference.

Of course, it was marvellous when Fred became a Christian. It was the start of a whole new life for us. But maybe your husband isn't a Christian, and you're all alone and fed up. That's how it was for me for many years. Here's the lessons I learned from my marriage, and not only how I learned to live with, but also, how to help my rough diamond . . .'

Doris has been married to her husband, Fred, for twenty-seven years. Fred Lemon's story is told in *Breakout*, and he has also written *Going Straight* and *Breakthrough*.

FREED FOR LIFE

Rita Nightingale

'Today, at round 11 am I got a twenty-year prison sentence. It didn't come as a shock, but it certainly came as a surprise. I was expecting over thirty . . .'

Prison Diary, 9 December 1977

Rita's sentence in Bangkok for drug-smuggling caused world-wide headlines. But the **real** story is how she became a Christian whilst in a Thai prison and how her life was transformed.

ORDER! ORDER!

Ramon Hunston

A scene in Parliament today. The Speaker, resplendent in his robes, subdues the unruly backbenchers . . . 'Order! Order!'

George Thomas now holds one of the highest posts in the land. His rise from the childhood poverty of the Welsh mining valleys, living with four brothers and sisters in a tiny Rhondda 'underhouse', is a remarkable testimony to his character, determination, and above all to his Christian faith. He explains to Ramon Hunston how it has weathered both the storms of doubt and the pressures of holding down one of the most demanding jobs which can be imagined. He relates it to his socialist commitment and his actions and attitudes in public life. As he says of himself—'It is amazing what God can do with a lad from the Rhondda with a patch on his trousers.'

TOWARDS CONFIRMATION

John Eddison

Why should I be confirmed? What does it mean?

This book explains how confirmation is a sign that you intend to walk as a Christian, and that God has accepted you as one of His Sons. It outlines the basics of the Christian faith and how it affects your day-to-day life. It helps you to understand one of the most important events in your life.